MW01094076

In Pursuit of
Glory

A Bible Study Rooted
in the Attributes of God

by Kelly Collier

Copyright © 2022 Behold Glory. All Rights Reserved.
Visit beholdglory.org for more Bible Studies & Resources.

ISBN: 978-1-959592-03-7

Formatting and cover design by Sarah Roberts of reflectingthedesigner.org

Unless specified, all Scripture quotations are from the ESV® Bible
(The Holy Bible, English Standard Version®), copyright © 2016 by Crossway,
a publishing ministry of Good News Publishers. Used by permission.
All rights reserved.

Table of Contents

You have said, "Seek my face."
My heart says to you, "Your face, LORD, do I seek."
Psalm 27:8

Before You Begin

For the next few months, we are going to dig into some rich verses about the character of our God. This kind of deeper digging into Scripture is formally known as the inductive study method. Don't let that fancy name scare you; inductive study is simply drawing out what is in the Scripture, allowing the Bible to speak for itself. It involves three steps: observation, interpretation, and application. With **observation** we are asking the question, *What does this passage say?* **Interpretation** takes us deeper as we ask, *What does this passage mean?* **Application** forces us to get personal and plan specific ways to change because of what we have learned. Our Bible study is not complete unless we ask ourselves, *What should I do?* Each month's lesson will guide you through the process of inductive Bible study. Just open your Bible, ask God to open your eyes, and then follow the steps laid out for you in the lesson.

If you are brand new to Bible study, you may feel a bit overwhelmed at the outset. This is not your typical fill-in-the-blank women's Bible study book. But please don't let all that empty space scare you. Bible study isn't complicated. God doesn't make it hard for us to get to know him. But it does take time and practice to develop your skills. God's glory is a treasure he doesn't share with the casual passer-by. But he delights to reveal himself to those who seek him earnestly. While true biblical meditation isn't complicated, neither is it easy. It requires the difficult discipline of being still and setting aside time to think about his truth. If, after reading the introduction, you don't understand how to do this study or just need some additional direction, please ask for help! Your small-group facilitator would be delighted to guide you through this process.

The inductive method isn't the *only* way to study the Bible. But it does give us a helpful framework for unpacking the truth of Scripture. Please don't get stuck on the "method" and miss the heart of Bible study: *knowing God*. By God's wise design we all have different capacities. Fight the tendency to compare with others. Simply do as much as you feel capable of doing. God will bless your dependent effort to seek after him.

To help us all get on the same page, our first group meeting will focus simply on becoming familiar with the elements of inductive study and learning how to use *The Tree*, a counseling tool developed by The Wilds. Before your first group meeting please read through the following introduction, *Changed by Glory*, which lays an important foundation for the study we are about to embark on together. As mentioned earlier, your group will then walk through the *Getting Started* section together at your first meeting.

In the appendix at the back of your notebook, you will find some additional helps:

- An introduction to *The Tree* along with several examples.
- A fuller explanation of *The Inductive Study Method*.
- While you don't need a lot of resources to be successful with this study, a list of *Word Study Tools* and *Suggested Resources* is provided for you in case you want some extra help along the way. For my personal Bible study, I simply use a piece of paper, a pen, and my Bible. Online Bible study websites prove helpful by providing easy access to word definitions, cross references, and commentaries.
- A *Study Example* for those who want to get a better idea of what this study looks like in action.

Since our focus is limited to one short passage each month, we are only scratching the surface concerning what our God is like. But I hope it whets your appetite for more! You can supplement your study by purchasing a good book on the attributes of God and reading the chapter that corresponds to the particular attribute you are studying in each lesson.

Back in the mid-seventies, J.I. Packer wrote a classic book on the character of God aptly titled *Knowing God*. The *Knowledge of the Holy* by A.W. Tozer and *God is More than Enough* by Jim Berg are also excellent choices. While a book isn't necessary, it can be an added blessing in your spiritual growth.

We have intentionally chosen some very familiar verses for our study. You might have memorized these verses as a young child or known them for more years than you can remember but never studied them in-depth. We can easily skim over these verses because they are so familiar and miss their potency, beauty, and practicality. When you come to a passage you think you already know well, or may have even studied in the past, ask the Lord to help you approach it with new eyes—and then be ready for a fresh feast from heaven. Our gracious Savior has invited us to know him. Let's set out together in *pursuit of glory*!

Lovingly in Christ,

Kelly Collier

Made in his Image

Making the transition from summer to fall in our family always includes the task of pulling out the jeans that haven't been worn all summer and having each child try on every pair to see what still fits and what needs to be passed down to younger friends. Working through the pile I noticed one particular pair because of the words printed on the tag: "Levi's 501 Jeans Made in the USA." The tag identifies both designer name and origin. Weber Grills, Wilson Footballs, Gibson Guitars, KitchenAid Mixers, Fiesta Tableware, Burt's Bees, Post-It Notes, and Crayola Crayons are just a few of the companies who still proudly stamp "Made in the USA" on their products. This identification seems to help these companies sell their product. Origin is important.

In a similar way, every human being has a tag, an identifying mark that reveals our Designer and origin, telling us who made us and where we came from.

> *So God created man in his own image, in the image of God he created him; male and female he created them.* (Genesis 1:27)

At creation God stamped his image on people. This is what identifies us as humans. Made by God. Made for God. Origin is important. God, our Designer and Creator, defines who we are and why we are here.

Image Bearers

Part of what it means to be image bearers of God is that we were designed to represent who God is and what he is like to the world. "The Hebrew word translated *image* is Tseh-lem. The exact same word used for images that ancient kings made to represent themselves throughout their kingdom."[1]

---

[1] *Made in God's Image*, video posted Nov. 4, 2015; https://answersingenesis.org/kids/videos/creation/made-gods-image/.

Imagine walking through the crowded streets of ancient Rome. Everywhere you looked you would see the image of Caesar: pressed into the face of the coins you bought and sold with, displayed on the statues that lined the streets, etched into the door of the temple erected for his worship. Caesar wanted his subjects to remember, all the time, that he was ruling on his throne. But he stole this idea from God.

Like a coin bearing the likeness of Caesar, each human being bears the likeness of God. Just as a coin or statue represented the greater reality of the living Caesar on his throne, our lives represent a much greater reality as well. God gave each of us the unique privilege and responsibility to represent him on earth—so that when we look at each other we can see something of our Creator and remember Who he is and what he is like. We were created to be little image bearers, pointing back to the ultimate reality of the living, ruling Creator God.

We are tasked with this important role: to demonstrate the beauty and worth of our great God to the world around us. As his image bearers, we are called to represent our King in a way that accurately reflects his character. This is what it means to "give glory" to God.[2] While all of creation displays God's glory (Ps. 19:1; Ps. 50:6; Rom. 1:19-20), humans alone were given the unique privilege of bearing his image. The One who is worthy of all glory created us for the purpose of bringing him glory (Rev. 4:11; Isa. 43:7; Eph. 1:6, 12; Col. 1:16).

Stolen Glory

But because of our condition as *fallen* image bearers of God, we fail to give God the glory he deserves. Instead we often steal glory for ourselves and provide a distorted representation of our Creator. Sin is our way of saying, "God, I don't want to be like You." Paul says in Romans 3:23, "for all have sinned and fall short of the glory of God." To "fall

---

[2] Giving glory to God has often been defined as "giving the right opinion of God."

short" means to be destitute or lacking in something. In this case, we are lacking in glory—God's glory. His image in us is marred by our sin. In our fallen condition, we cannot fully bring him the glory that he deserves.

The Gospel
Enter the good news. The gospel—the good news of God's saving work through Christ's atoning death and life-giving resurrection—tells us how we can move from *fallen* to *forgiven*, setting us on a course of being accurate glory bearers once again.. When we are justified by faith in Christ, God gives believers a righteous standing before him. God sees us just as he sees his Son: righteous, complete, holy. Glory restored. So, our aim is glory. But spend a day at my house and you will agree with me that we are not very glorious creatures. We live in the messy "here and now." We live with the daily reality of "sin which clings so closely" (Heb. 12:1) and the suffering that comes from living in a broken world. The distance between the day of our adoption into God's family and the day of our placement with him in glory can seem interminable. It's all too easy to lose sight of God's promises. The hope of glory seems so far off.

The Hope of Glory
When we talk about the *"hope of glory,"* what do we really mean? Paul references this hope in several of his letters. In Romans 5:2 we learn that it is only through Christ that we have *"obtained access by faith into this grace in which we stand,"* which leads us to be able to *"rejoice in hope of the glory of God."* Believers stand in grace, having been placed by God into a secure, unchanging union with Jesus. We are in Christ—justified through his death and resurrection. Our sins have been forgiven, and we are declared righteous by God. This is an amazing gift! There is nothing we could ever do to remove our guilty record. Christ has done it for us! We rejoice in the knowledge of this truth. As Martin-Lloyd Jones said when commenting on this passage, "If you are justified you can be assured that you are going to be sanctified and glorified. Nothing can come between us and this guaranteed

end." Glory is certain. One day we will perfectly represent our Creator God. We will "be like him" (1 Jn. 3:2). We stand "in him" and, no matter how unlike Jesus we look today, our union with Christ is our hope of glory.

Union with Christ

But union with Christ means more than this. Not only are we declared forgiven, we are swept up into the very life of Christ, joined to him in a living union. Jesus is our sanctification (1 Cor. 1:30). In Colossians 1:27 Paul says that *"the hope of glory"* is *"Christ in you."* Believers are in Christ, but Christ is also in the believer. This means that every believer shares in the righteous life of Christ. This reality is literally "our hope of glory." As *forgiven* image bearers, we are set on an inevitable course of *becoming Christ-like* image bearers.[3] Inevitable, because this is the end result for all who are "in Christ."

But also a course because this is a journey of growth that will continue throughout our lives. Sanctification is the process of the righteous life of Jesus becoming more and more of a reality in our daily experience. It takes place between the "now" of our justification and the "not yet" of our glorification. One day we will be like Jesus. "Christ in you" is our assurance that this promise will be fulfilled.

Already. Not Yet.

The apostle John demonstrates both aspects of our union with Christ in 1 John 3:1-3. These three verses are a beautiful summary of the gospel. John reminds his readers that they are forgiven and justified.

Beloved, we are God's children now. (1 John 3:2a)

Believers enter this new relationship as God's children at a point in the past, but it has ongoing results. Believers belong to God. The sin problem that kept us from a relationship

---

[3] Some of the phrasing I use in this section comes from a personal conversation with Dr. Jim Berg.

with God has been taken care of—Christ took our sinful record and bore our penalty. We were given Christ's righteous record and brought into the family, adopted as God's own child. Justified and adopted. Before, we were his enemies; now we have the privilege of calling God our Father. There is an important word in verse 2 that we need to consider: *now*. This emphasizes a point in time. Right now, already, we are God's children. We need to repeat this often, especially because the "family likeness" isn't often readily seen.

Thankfully, God is not finished with his children. The word "now" stands in contrast with the "not yet" that comes later in the verse. We find this "already, not yet" tension often in Paul's writings. Our adoption has already occurred in a legal sense and we enjoy many of its privileges, but there is a "not yet" aspect to our salvation, something yet to anticipate.

> *...and what we will be has not yet appeared; but we know that when he appears we shall be like him, because we shall see him as he is. (1 John 3:2b)*

There is something hidden about every child of God, something that has not yet been revealed. This same word describes how Jesus made God known when he "appeared" (Tit. 2:11, 3:4; Jn. 2:11). In this verse, the word "appear" is in the passive voice, meaning someone else is going to cause our true nature as God's children to be known. We are not going to do it to ourselves. We don't have that kind of power. "What we will be has not yet appeared." This new state of being will take place in the future. It does not mean that our fundamental nature will change—just that what we *really* are as believers will be fully revealed. The word "what" suggests that it will be something inconceivably glorious. What is this glorious mystery about us that will someday be revealed? One day we will "be like him." We will be of the same nature as Jesus himself. When he returns, we will be transformed fully and finally into his image. We will perfectly reflect the glory of the Creator.

Creation. Fall. Redemption!

This really gets to the heart of what redemption is all about. God created man in his own likeness. That likeness was distorted by sin. Redemption is God's plan to restore us to his perfect image once again.

If "what we are" speaks of our justification, then "what we will be" speaks of our future glorification. We will become glorified children of God. This is the future condition that awaits all true believers! John says this is something we can "know" with absolute confidence. Even though Christ's perfect nature has not been fully realized in our lives yet and our current struggle with sin seems to contradict this truth, we *know* he will keep this promise. We will be like him. God will not fail at this task (Philippians 1:6).

The Process of Transformation

But let's consider how God intends to accomplish this task: *when he appears we shall be like him, because we shall see him as he is.* John is referring to the events recorded in the book of Revelation—the second coming of Jesus, when he returns in resplendent, unveiled glory. At his first coming, Jesus kept his glory mostly veiled. But on *this* future day we will "see him as he is." To "see" means to look on, to behold; it has the idea of being an eyewitness. We will be like him *because* we see him. God's glory is so powerful it will change us the instant we see him face to face. This vision of Christ is what completes the transformation in all believers—the transformation that was begun at the new birth. We will finally become like him when we see him in this ultimate sense. This isn't something we can perceive with our physical eyes right now; it is a promise we receive by faith. And notice John's language: not "if" but "when." When he appears, we will be like him. We *already* are the children of God. But we don't even fully realize what this means. What is already true of us will be fully revealed one day. Even though we will change significantly, the essence of what we are will remain the same for all eternity—beloved children of God.

In verse 2 we see both our **justification** (what we are) and our **glorification** (what we shall be). Now...not yet. What do we do with the space between the now and the not yet? The beautiful truths of justification and future glorification have incredible implications for how we live right now as believers.

> *And everyone who thus hopes in him purifies himself as he is pure. (1 John 3:3)*

Salvation is not simply a past event that will benefit us someday in the distant future. Salvation is a present tense reality. John deals with our **sanctification** in this verse— God's saving work in our lives in the present.

What is true of genuine believers who have fixed their hope on Christ? They *purify* themselves. The word *purify* comes from the root word hagias, meaning "holy" (see Ja. 4:8; 1 Tim. 5:22; 2 Cor. 7:11, 11:2). This verb is in the present tense, indicating the ongoing personal effort involved. Notice the standard: *as he is pure*. Jesus is the standard. We are called to mirror his purity in our lives. God wants his children to be like Jesus—image bearers who reflect his purity and holiness.

Don't miss it: Everyone who has *this hope* of becoming like Jesus one day will apply themselves to become like Jesus right now. Far from being motivated by obligation or a desire to gain God's approval, a believer should be motivated to action by hope.

Dependent Obedience

John is telling us that we must be active in cleansing our lives from sin—and we are to do this continually, without letting up. This involves personal effort. Hope-filled believers are occupied with becoming holy while we are on this earth. But please don't misinterpret John's teaching. When scripture calls us to personal effort, it is not calling us to a self-dependent effort but, rather, effort that is empowered by the Holy Spirit. We have a personal responsibility for our progress in godliness. But we also understand that any progress we make is only possible through divine enablement. God does the changing, but we have the privilege of cooperating with him in this sanctifying work. In our home we like to call it "dependent obedience." As we go through life, we should look less and less like our naturally sinful selves and more and more like the glorified saints we are destined to become.

How do we cooperate with God in what he is doing to make us like his Son? Do you remember what John says will complete our transformation? Beholding Christ in his unveiled glory—when we see him face to face. So, cooperating with God towards this end has everything to do with seeing him now. God uses the same means for our transformation in the present as he will use in the future: *beholding his glory*.

Getting Glory from God

Paul picks up this same theme in 2 Corinthians 3. Throughout this chapter, Paul refers to an encounter Moses had with God. You can read the story in Exodus 33. Moses made a bold request of God: "Please show me your glory." From the context we learn that Moses was not asking for a personal experience for himself; he was really interceding on behalf of the people God had called him to lead. He desperately wanted God to be with his people Israel.

God answered Moses' request. The next morning Moses made the long trek back up the mountain. God took Moses and put him in an opening in the mountainside, covering him with his hand. Then God passed by, declaring his name and his character to Moses. After passing by, he removed his hand and allowed Moses to see just the passing remnants of his glory. And Moses was radically changed. Exodus 34:29 says that "the skin of his face shone because he had been talking with God." Seeing God's glory literally changed him. The light of God's glory glowed on the face of Moses.

In 2 Corinthians, Paul uses this familiar story to make a strong contrast between the Old and New Covenants. The Old Covenant, the law given on Mount Sinai, has its own form of glory. The law reveals God's character. But the law cannot transform. It can only condemn. This is what God designed it to do—to show us our need for a Savior. But it cannot change hearts. In contrast, the New Covenant has a different kind of glory – a far greater glory. The New Covenant, the ministry of the Spirit in the lives of those who trust in Christ, brings true transformation. In Moses' day, Israel's heart was hard—or Paul uses the word "veiled." They couldn't even look at the after-effects of God's glory on Moses' face because of their unbelief. But this dark veil of unbelief is removed through faith in Christ so that we are able to see God's glory. Nothing hinders our vision anymore. This is the context for 2 Corinthians 3:18.

> *And we all, with unveiled face, beholding the glory of the Lord, are being transformed into the same image from one degree of glory to another. For this comes from the Lord who is the Spirit.*

Beholding
We find two notable verbs in this passage. Beholding means to see reflected in a mirror; "to gaze with wide-open eyes, as at something remarkable." There is nothing passive or casual about this word; it has the idea of an intense, earnest, and continued inspection of something. It describes the person who has a deep longing to see God. We "behold" God in his Word. His Word acts like a mirror—reflecting his character, his glory, on every page. This verb belongs to us. We are responsible to behold the glory of the Lord.

Transformed
The second important verb, *are being transformed*, means to transform. Our English word "metamorphosis" comes from this Greek word. This verb belongs to God. He changes us as we behold his glory. Another amazing truth we learn from this verb: it is in the present tense, meaning it is something

that God does continually in our lives. In this verse, God's action toward those who behold his glory is stated as a fact. This is what God is continually doing in every believer who beholds him in his Word. Notice the end goal of the transformation: changed *into the same image*. We become like what we behold. This means, as we behold his image, we become more like him by degrees. God gives us some of his glory. God further emphasizes his work in this process with the phrase, "for this comes from the Lord who is the Spirit." Far from changing by self-effort on demand, this process describes God's work to make us like Jesus by the power of his Spirit. Jim Berg summarizes this well: "The Spirit of God uses the Word of God to make me like the Son of God. No one who is exposed to the glories of God as they are revealed by God's Spirit through the Scriptures will remain the same." The result of beholding God—seeing his glory in his Word— is change. The glory of God is that powerful! As we behold him, we are changed *from one degree of glory to another*— little by little we will grow to reflect more and more of his character. This process takes place over time. One day we will be like him when we see him in his unveiled glory. But even before that great day, and precisely because of that great hope, we can become more like him by seeking that glory now.

Our Greatest Responsibility
We could make the case, then, that beholding God in his Word is our biggest responsibility as Christians. While we can't see God with our physical eyes like Moses, we can humbly pray Moses' prayer and then set out to see God in the Bible. By seeing him we are made like him. God has chosen his Word to be the main tool he uses to transform us. We cannot grow to become Christ-like image bearers of God without it. Do you see how the believer's responsibility to behold God is tied directly to our created purpose?

Years ago I heard evangelist Steve Pettit describe his personal time with the Lord each day as his time to "get glory from God." What an excellent description of what is really happening when we dependently open our Bibles to behold our God! This view of Scripture takes "having devotions" to an entirely different level. God never intended us to approach his Word as a task we must accomplish on our daily spiritual checklist. Beholding God is far more glorious than simply looking for spiritual advice to help us make it through the day. **The Bible is all about a Person.**

It's All About God!

I remember when I first began to borrow this prayer from Moses to use as my own. Early on in our marriage, Matt and I read a book that challenged us to slow the pace of our Bible study and begin to look for more than a "word of encouragement" or a "principle to live by" but, rather, to begin looking for a Person.[4] Up to that point in my Christian life, though consistent, my "devotions" had mostly been about principles and lessons I could learn from Scripture. Principles aren't bad, but the Bible is so much more than just principles. God wanted us to go deeper during our time in his Word, to pursue something far richer than mere spiritual principles to live by. God showed us that day that the Bible was all about him. That may seem really obvious, but somehow along the way I had missed it. And my time in God's Word took on a whole new purpose. The God of heaven was inviting me to know *him*! What an awesome and humbling invitation.

We took up the challenge we were given to stay in one place in Scripture until the truth really began to change us.[5] If the whole Bible is about God, then *every* narrative story, *every* command in the Law, *every* line of biblical poetry, *every* prophetic utterance, and *every* New Testament letter reveals his character. But God's character is not always easy to spot. So instead of jumping right into more challenging parts like Leviticus, Matt and I decided to start with passages where God visibly revealed himself to people. We figured that

---

[4] Berg, Jim. *Changed Into his Image*. Greenville: Journey Forth, 1999, p.124.
[5] Ibid, see chapter 6.

when God shows up like that, it's pretty hard to miss truth about him! Our first passage was Genesis 15. We spent that whole summer digging deep into this encounter between Abram and God. We made a commitment not to move on until the Lord had shown us something about himself and we were changed by it. What we were learning about God was often the topic of our conversations. We grew so much that summer! I still remember when the Lord "turned the light on" for both of us and how seeing God's glory in Genesis 15 impacted our thinking about life and the specific trials we were facing at the time. An amazing side benefit was that, as we grew closer to the Lord, we also grew closer to each other. We have seen the same benefit in our small-group Bible studies over the years. I love being in the lobby of our church building on Sunday morning and catching portions of conversations about what different women are learning from God's Word. Beholding God together builds a powerful unity and comradery!

The Renewing Guide
After several years of studying Old Testament passages where God visually revealed himself to people, we decided to take a new turn in our study on God's character and begin working through *The Renewing Guide*.[6] This guide is designed to help show the connection between our more obvious outward sins and our less obvious inward sins of unbelief. Christ used the familiar image of a tree to illustrate an important truth about people (Mt. 7:15-20; Lk. 6:43-49).[7] Just as a tree shows its nature by the fruit it produces, the inner nature of a person—what he wants and what he believes—is revealed by the fruit—the actions and words—produced in his life.

This illustration proves helpful because it reveals that biblical change can't happen by simply trying to change

---

[6] *The Renewing Guide* is a counseling tool developed by The Wilds; used with permission.

[7] For a more thorough explanation of The Tree refer to the appendix.

fruit—taking off the bad and replacing it with good. Ken Collier states it this way: "The things that you are doing wrong **prove** that you do not know your God as you should. Each *bad fruit* indicates that you are actually attacking the things that are always true about God by not believing the truths about him enough to act on them. You do not really believe something until you believe it enough to act on it." Knowing God is essential to biblical change. Since the root of every sin is *unbelief,* changing the character of our "tree" means we must know and *believe* the truth about God.

The study that follows is designed to help us work out this renewing process on a personal level (Eph. 4:22-24). As we have already seen, beholding the glory of God is the most important aspect of biblical change. As we "behold" him in his Word, we are gradually changed to reflect his glory. We can see God on every page of Scripture. Through the enabling power of the Holy Spirit, we can approach God's Word with this *glory-driven* mindset.

With the humble boldness of Moses, we can ask God to allow us the privilege of beholding his excellent character. An open Bible and a tender heart position us for God to work in our lives. The result will be lives that increasingly reflect his character and bring him glory. "Getting glory from God" enables us to "give glory" to God.

God is Not Hiding
Our youngest son loves to play active games with the family. Among his all-time favorites: flashlight hide and seek. Best played in winter when darkness falls earlier in the evenings, we turn out all the lights in the house and give everyone a flashlight. The appointed seeker begins to count and everyone else scurries to find a place to hide.

Please don't tell Levi, but searching for a kid with a flashlight who has a hard time ever being quiet is not that challenging—just listen for the muffled giggles coming from the bathroom laundry hamper. He just can't stand it. He wants to be found. Unlike a young child, if God wanted to hide from us, we would not be able to find him. But God is not playing a game of cosmic hide and seek with his creation. It is God's disposition to be known. He isn't hiding. He wants to be found.

Relationship: To Know and Be Known
The opening chapters of the Bible reveal this truth to us. God made us for relationship with him. Made in his image, we were designed to know and be known by our Creator God (Gen. 1:26). Relationship was God's idea. God himself is relational: Father, Son, and Holy Spirit. And God made us relational—it is one of the distinct ways that we bear his image. In his book, *From the Garden to the City*, John Dyer put it this way: "God originally designed humans to function in a deeply interdependent way that reflects the tri-personhood of God" (p. 45). Your inner desire to draw near to God and others in relationship was put there by God.

Just in case we miss God's desire to connect deeply with us in the opening chapters of the Bible, he goes on to clearly tell us of his intention throughout the pages of Scripture. We find it everywhere—in the Prophets, the Psalms, the books of the Law, and on into the New Testament (for several examples see: Lev. 26:11-12; Isa. 57:15; Jer. 24:7; Jn. 1:10-12, 14; Jn. 17:3). God invites people into relationship with him.

The Obstacle of Sin
But this is where we run into difficulty. We face several serious obstacles to knowing God in this way. First, we must face the reality that God is holy and we are sinful. God isn't hiding from us, but when Adam and Eve sinned, mankind began to hide from God (Gen. 3:10). Our sin separates us from God and shuts us out from a relationship with him.

God's Merciful Solution
In his lovingkindness, God has provided the solution. He opened the way through Jesus. God doesn't invite good people who have their lives together to come and experience

his mercy. God invites only sinners, those who know they are "sick" (Mk. 2:17). We see this in the book of Jeremiah when God speaks these words to his chosen people during a time when they had gone far away from him:

> *"You will seek me and find me, when you seek me with all your heart. I will be found by you, declares the LORD." (Jer. 29:13-14a)*

His disposition toward sinners has remained the same throughout history: sinful people invited by God to seek and find him. This is good news!

How to Know God
Secondly, in the words of a familiar hymn, God is "glorious, indescribable." How can an infinite God be known? And yet, he has made himself known. While we can behold certain aspects of his nature from the creation he has made (Rom. 1:19-20), we cannot *know* God apart from his Word. The Bible is the way God has chosen to reveal Who he is and what he is like. And even more specifically, John records in his gospel, *"And the Word became flesh and dwelt among us, and we have seen his glory, glory as of the only Son from the Father, full of grace and truth"* (Jn. 1:14). Moses' prayer (*Please show me Your glory*) was answered in the ultimate sense when Jesus took on flesh. Through Jesus we behold the glory of God most clearly.[8] Jesus was the perfect image bearer. He represented God perfectly.

As you well know, the entire Bible tells the story of God's mission to restore mankind's ability to know and relate to him through Jesus Christ. Far from hiding and retreating from his rebellious creation, God became like his creation—taking on *our likeness* so that we could be restored to *his likeness* (Jn. 1:14; Phil. 2:7). From the Garden of Eden to the New Jerusalem, God actively draws near to mankind, redeeming us from our miserable condition of sin and

---

[8] Because of this reality, we will take some time in each lesson to consider how Jesus revealed the attribute of God that we are studying in his earthly life.

restoring us to the likeness of his Son. In the final book of the Bible we find the culmination of redemptive history: a people saved and transformed by God's grace, gathered around the throne to "worship him" (Rev. 22:3). Revelation 21:3 describes what the new heavens and the new earth will be like: "Behold, the dwelling place of God is with man. He will dwell with them, and they will be his people, and God himself will be with them as their God." The most important aspect of heaven is that God is there. And his redeemed people are with him. A relationship unhindered by sin. This is God's intended end of all his saving work. Can you imagine the delight of unhindered, intimate fellowship with God that Adam and Eve once enjoyed? We will know this joy one day. And we will know it eternally!

Isn't it humbling to consider that the God of the universe wants you to know him? What would compel him to draw near to us—the rebels, enemies, and sinners that we are? We could summarize the answer to this question in one word: *glory*. God's glory. The ultimate end of God's redeeming work is his glory. He is glorified by pouring out the riches of his grace on undeserving sinners, lavishing them with his love; forgiving, redeeming, and restoring people simply because he is a God who delights in mercy (Eph. 1:3-12).

Glorification
There is so much hope in understanding God's disposition toward us as sinners. We know where we are headed. We know how the story will end. One day we will reflect his image perfectly. Never again will we weep with sorrow or sigh with regret over our failure to properly reflect his glory in our lives. God will accomplish what he has started and make us like his Son (Phil. 1:6, 1 Jn. 3:1-3; 1 Pt. 5:10)! But along with tremendous hope, knowing God's intended end for our lives also gives us direction. We have something toward which we can clearly aim during our days between the present and the future. We can spend our lives *in pursuit of glory*.

*Thus saith the Lord, "Let not the wise man glory in his wisdom, neither let the mighty man glory in his might, let not the rich man glory in his riches: **But let him that glorieth glory in this, that he understandeth and knoweth me, that I am the Lord** which exercise lovingkindness, judgment, and righteousness, in the earth: for in these things I delight," saith the Lord.*

Jeremiah 9:23-24, KJV

For Discussion:

1. How is God's saving work in your life (past, present, and future) directly related to his glory? What does God's glory have to do with your **justification**? What role does God's glory play in your **sanctification**? How does God's glory relate to your **glorification**?

2. How does remembering the gospel and your union with Christ impact both your motivation and enablement to change? How do these truths give hope especially when dealing with an area of entrenched sin in your life?

3. 1 John clearly teaches that we are living between the *now* of our justification and the *not yet* of our glorification. What does 1 John 3:3 assume God's children will do with the space in between? What should this practically look like in your own life (1 Jn 3:3; 2 Cor. 3:18)?

4. How does change happen in the life of the believer? Who is responsible for the sanctification process? God or you? Explain your answer.

5. Beholding God's glory literally made Moses' face glow (Ex. 34:29). How do believers behold God's glory today? What impact does God promise will result in their lives (2 Cor. 3:18)?

6. All of us have times when we experience a gap between what we *feel* to be true and what is *actually* true, when we struggle to think and live Bible. Practically, how should knowing the truth about God (Who God is and what he says) inform our feelings and help us move back toward reality again.

Getting Started

"Our aim in studying the Godhead
must be to know God Himself better.
Our concern must be to enlarge our
acquaintance, not simply with the
doctrine of God's attributes, but with the
living God whose attributes they are."

J.I. Packer

What is an Attribute of God?

Over the centuries, many gifted theologians have set out to answer this question.[9] For the sake of simplicity, we will use A.W. Tozer's definition from his classic book, *The Knowledge of the Holy*:

> "An attribute of God is whatever God has in any way revealed as being true of himself."[10]

God has revealed himself to us in his Word, which means that the Bible is our source for discovering truth about him. Remember, the Bible is all about a Person!

From our limited human perspective we tend to think of attributes as individual parts that make up the whole of a person, like a set of ingredients listed on a recipe. But that isn't how it works with God at all. A.W. Tozer goes on to say, "An attribute...is not a part of God. It is *how* God is, and as far as the reasoning mind can go, we may say that it is *what* God is."[11]

> "The divine attributes are what we know to be true of God. He does not possess them as qualities; they are how God is as he reveals himself to his creatures. Love, for instance, is not something God has and which may grow or diminish or cease to be. His love is the way God is, and when he loves he is simply being himself. And so with the other attributes."[12]

This is a little hard to wrap our minds around! But remembering this guards us from isolating one attribute of God from another. Each of his attributes are ***always* true** about him (e.g., God is unchanging in his wisdom; he cannot become more or less wise). God possesses each of his

---

[9] The Attributes of God are usually included in The Doctrine of God section in systematic theology books.

[10] Tozer, A.W. *The Knowledge of the Holy*. New York: Harper & Row Publishers, 1961, p.20.

[11] Ibid, p.23.

[12] Ibid, p.24.

attributes in **perfection** (e.g., God is perfectly wise). Each of his attributes are in **perfect harmony** with the others (e.g., God's wisdom is never at odds with his love).

We also must remember that God's attributes are true whether we acknowledge them as true or not. An individual may declare a lack of belief in the law of gravity, but that does not change the reality of gravity on that individual's life when he attempts skydiving without a parachute. God is who he says he is. Our ignorance or complete rejection of God's declared truth does not change reality.

Teach Me Your Way, Lord

Theologians historically categorize God's attributes under two main headings: those which are communicable and those which are not. For example, God alone is supreme and omniscient. To these non-communicable attributes, we must simply respond to God in trust, worship, and humble submission. And while our response to his communicable attributes should certainly be the same, we can add to it the desire expressed by the psalmist, "Teach me your way, O LORD" (Ps. 27:11). Like David, we can cultivate a desire to grow in becoming a better image bearer so that we more accurately reflect his glorious nature (e.g., although we will never be all-wise like God, we can grow in wisdom). Again, for the sake of simplicity, we are using the more intimate child-like headings in our study: *God is Great* and *God is Good.* I think we would all agree that there is a lot of theology packed into that simple children's prayer.

This Side Up

Appliances usually come in a box marked "this side up." The label on the box is intended to minimize any damage to the product during the shipping process. When studying God's attributes, we can avoid "damage" by keeping things right side up. We have this habit of attempting to turn things upside down by putting ourselves at the center of our Bible study.

We already defined an attribute of God as something that is *true about him*, but we have a tendency to define God by what is *true about us*. Sinclair Ferguson makes this point well in his book Devoted to God:[13]

> Any description we give of what God is like in himself—in technical terms, describing his 'attributes'—must meet a simple test. For anything to be true of God as he is in himself it must be true quite apart from his work of creation, quite apart from our existence or even the existence of angels, archangels, cherubim and seraphim. It must be true of God simply as he always existed as the eternal Trinity.

God's attributes are what is true of him even apart from us. In fact, we can go so far as to say that we aren't even part of the definition. Like the Bible, God's attributes are all about *him*—not us. And yet, God graciously invites us into relationship with him. And in his kind wisdom, knowing how much we struggle to relate to what we can't see with our eyes or touch with our hands, he chooses to relate to us in images that we can understand.

It is hard for us to grasp what it means that God is Omniscient, Omnipresent, and Immutable. And so, he gives us images to which we can relate. He calls himself names like Savior, Judge, Creator, Father, Shepherd, Friend, Healer, Husband, and King. God wants us to know what it means that he is merciful, and so he calls himself our Savior—giving us an idea of how he relates to us because of his attribute of mercy. From this same title we learn that he is *able* to save because he is the Almighty God. And we learn that he *wants* to save because of his attribute of love. God speaks to us in images to help us understand his unchanging attributes.

God's attributes are unchangingly true about him. But how he relates to people does change based on the state of their

---

[13] Ferguson, Sinclair. *Devoted to God: Blueprints for Sanctification.* East Peoria: Versa Press, Inc., 2016, pp.1-2.

relationship with him. While God will always be a God of justice, how we experience his justice depends entirely on our standing in Christ. God's does not stop being just and simply decide to overlook sin when a person trusts Jesus Christ as their Savior. God's justice is satisfied in the work of Christ on the behalf of the repentant sinner, while those who remain outside of Christ will experience God's justice to the full extent when they stand before him on judgment day.

We are glory seekers. This desire for glory speaks to our creation design. But remember, we are fallen image bearers and our desire for glory is seriously corrupted. God designed us for *his* glory. Everything about us was designed to loop back to him and bring him glory. We run the danger, even as believers who deeply desire to glorify God, of falling short in our aims of glory. Even as we study the character of God and are blessed by the change it brings in our lives, we must remember that this study isn't about us. By God's grace, we can keep God at the center of the story as we study his Word in the months to come.

Pursuing Glory

We realize that, as mere mortals with limited knowledge, we cannot ever say that we fully know God. But with what he has made known to us about himself, through his Word, we can become intimately familiar with him. He has invited us to do just that!

In high school I ran on our local high school track team. I was best at short-distance races and never got into the endurance training required for cross-country running. Just once, when I was about 13, I ran a half-marathon. The course was laid out through downtown Honolulu and ended with a grand finish at Aloha Stadium. There are only a few times in my short life that I have felt like I came close to death. And this was one of them. With a long-distance race, the course laid out can seem so insurmountable that one can be tempted to give up before even getting started. But I reached the finish line that day, one step at a time.

Pursuing glory is like that. Knowing God can seem like such an insurmountable task. But the road "from glory to glory" (2 Cor. 3:18, KJV) requires just one step at a time. The study to follow is designed to help us take *one more step* in getting to know the God who has called us into relationship with himself.

This one little notebook doesn't even have room for us to explore all of the attributes of God, much less all of the verses in Scripture that reveal the attributes we are taking time to consider. While I have sought to pick passages for us to study that give us a good view of God's glory, no one passage of Scripture can fully capture the multi-faceted splendor of any one of God's attributes. But it is a beginning. The goal of this study is simply to help you practice a pattern. Just one verse, prayerfully studied and applied. One step. Knowing how to nurture your relationship with God, how to behold his glory in the Word, and how to apply it personally gives you a pattern you can keep following until you reach the finish line.

What we believe about God...that is where it all starts. And that is where true biblical change must start too. Faith is foundational to the Christian life—belief in who God is and what he has said. All sin finds its roots in unbelief. This is why A.W. Tozer said, "What comes into our minds when we think about God is the most important thing about us...A right conception of God is basic...to practical Christian living." The choices we make in our lives are the direct result of what we believe about God. It is truly the most important thing about us.

How to Do this Study

Each lesson will follow the simple format below, in which we will seek to:

Memorize

- Commit the attribute, definition, and corresponding verse to memory.

Meditate

- Prayerfully meditate on the supplied verse(s). Use the inductive study method as a guide at whatever degree you feel comfortable.

- Journal your answers to the meditation questions that are provided.

- Add additional verses that you discover on your own which communicate the same truth about God's character.

Apply

- Make personal application to your own life. How does beholding this particular aspect of God's glory change you?

- Use *The Tree* diagram to "counsel yourself."

Share

- Talk to God about what you are learning through prayer.

- Share what you are learning with another believer.

While these steps are simple and self-explanatory, the next few pages expand further on what each step entails.

Memorize

True meditation requires memorization. Taking time to learn God's words by heart allows us to call them back to mind all day long. What does a whole-hearted pursuit of God look like? According to Psalm 119:11, it certainly includes hiding God's Word in our hearts—a process that begins with memorization.

Meditate

Prayerfully meditate on the supplied verse(s). A merely academic study of the Bible won't change you, but a humble and dependent one will! We best express our dependence on God through prayer, admitting our need for him to open the "eyes of [our] heart" to understand his truth (Eph. 1:18). This is vital because we cannot understand spiritual truth apart from his enabling (Ps. 119:18; Lk. 24: 44-45; 1 Jn. 5:20). Begin prayerfully, and then continue prayerfully. Carry this same spirit of humble dependence throughout your time of **study** and **meditation**. Remember, we aren't studying to fill up empty space in a notebook; we are seeking to get to know a Person. Pray that God will use your time in his Word to nurture your relationship with him.

The **meditation questions** provide an opportunity to explore **how each attribute of God is attributed to Jesus or displayed in his earthly life.** We see God's character revealed most clearly in the Person of his Son, Jesus Christ (Isa. 40:5). Jesus came to reveal God to us—to make him known. By looking at Jesus, especially during his earthly ministry, we can learn a lot about who God is and what he is like. In addition, you will also seek to **identify one Bible example** (positive or negative) of a person who demonstrated either belief or unbelief in each attribute of God by the way they chose to live. In a way, we are already getting into application in this step. Thinking through real-life examples provided in Scripture helps us see the vital nature of our beliefs. As A.W. Tozer once said, "What you believe about God is the most important thing about you." What we believe—or don't believe—in great measure determines the outcome of our lives.

To **find other verses** about a particular attribute of God use the concordance in the back of your Bible, cross references listed in the margin of your Bible, or the search feature on an online Bible program such as <u>blueletterbible.org</u>. Adding to your collection of truth about God will give you a whole sheet of verses you can use in prayer and worship. Remember, beholding his glory should lead us to worship the glorious God we behold!

Apply

Personally, I think **application** is the hardest part of Bible study. Often uncomfortable, and always humbling, we can be tempted to skip over this important step. But without it, we run the danger of becoming spiritually proud and deceiving ourselves into thinking we have learned great things when, in reality, we leave our study of God's Word unchanged (1 Cor. 8:1; Ja. 1:22-25).

Think of the various people in Scripture who encountered God's glory in a personal way. Moses. Daniel. The Apostle John. Peter, James, and John. In each encounter, the one doing the beholding ends up bowed down before the awesome presence of God. When we truly behold the glorious character of our God, it will humble us. We will bow. This is the only proper response to glory.

Personal application requires us to ask some honest questions of ourselves: Do I need to repent of any ways in which I have sought to rob God of glory? What needs to change in my life so that I glorify God by believing what he has said about himself in his Word? How should beholding this particular aspect of God's glory change me?

Even as you humble yourself before the Lord and allow him to shine the light of his Word into your life, don't forget that you have much to praise him for. God is so kind to bring conviction—it is one of the most loving things he does in our lives. We would not see a doctor as being good or kind if he held back knowledge of a potentially fatal sickness simply to spare our feelings. As Jerry Bridges says, "It is always a good thing when God humbles us." He understands so much better than we do the incredibly destructive nature of sin.

We want to be like Jesus. But reality often doesn't match our desire. We often fail to give God the glory for which he is worthy. This is why it is so important to remember the gospel, to "preach it to ourselves everyday" as Jerry Bridges so often admonishes in his writings. We never can and never will merit God's favor by how well we perform. As believers we never have to fear the loss of our righteous standing before God. We will *always* and *only* relate to God through Jesus, on the basis of his finished work on our behalf. And this means that we are free to face our sin because we don't ever have to fear facing God's wrath.

Approach personal application with this gospel perspective. Seek forgiveness and then rejoice that forgiveness has already been freely granted to you because of Jesus and his work on your behalf. Allow conviction to remind you of God's gracious disposition toward you as a Father and not a Judge. He is keeping his promise to save you from sin and make you more like Jesus. And we can go one step further by taking time to consider how God has shown this particular aspect of his character to us personally. God is not only good, he is good to *us*. Respond in worship to God for what he has shown you about himself!

Personal application also requires us to think deeply about positive action steps that need to take place in our lives. Often our time in the Word will reveal things we need to stop doing, but we certainly shouldn't leave it there. Growth is positive—and we need to ask ourselves how we can actively become better image bearers of God. We sin in and with our physical bodies. In the same way, obedience will be seen in our bodies—in our thoughts, affections, words, and actions.

But again, when we begin talking about what we must do, we run the risk of defaulting to self-effort, performance-oriented living. Because of this tendency, it is vital that we approach action steps of obedience with a gospel perspective as well. The gospel reminds us that just as Christ died in our place, he also obeyed in our place. He is our justification and he is our sanctification. Becoming like Jesus means far more than mere imitation. Becoming like Jesus means that his life *in* us becomes more and more of a reality in our daily experience (Gal. 2:20). Keep your union with Christ front and center in your thinking as you apply steps for biblical change in your life. James Stuart put it well: "Only when union with Christ is kept central is sanctification seen in its true nature as the unfolding of Christ's own character within the believer's life."

Faith will work out in our lives. We must obey. But we can't obey apart from the power of the Holy Spirit. "Only as we understand that God's acceptance of us is based on grace can we respond to a challenge to pursue holiness without falling into a performance mindset" (Jerry Bridges). Union with Christ enables and motivates obedience in the life of the believer. Gratitude propels us to serve our gracious Savior and King. Even as you ask God to show you what action steps you need to take, humbly express your dependence on him. Dependent obedience: this is how you cooperate with his Spirit as he works in you to make you more like Jesus. When we pray, "teach me Your way, Lord," (Ps. 25:4; 27:11) he will answer!

"With my whole heart I seek You" (Ps. 119:10). The Palmist made this important decision because he was aware of the blessing attached to seeking God in this way (v. 2). A "whole heart" includes the mind, affections, and will. Seeking God with our whole heart means that we submit to his Word as authoritative in our lives— believing what he says, loving and valuing what he says, and engaging our wills to obey what he says. Like the psalmist, we too can know the blessing of a whole-hearted response to God.

The last step in the application section is to **use *The Tree* diagram to "counsel yourself."** *The Tree* is a visual tool designed to help us personally apply what we are learning about God. If you are unfamiliar with *The Tree*, please read the explanatory section provided in the appendix. Using this simple tool can help us see the connection between our sin and our unbelief. It is my prayer that, as we get to know God better, we will learn to trust him and then act on what we know to be true. As we cooperate with what he is doing in us, our lives will bear more of the "good" fruit that reflects his character and brings glory to his name.

Share

As we saw in the application section, good theology will always produce humility and gratitude. We express these heart attitudes in worship—through prayer and praise. Take time to **respond to God**, praising him for who he is and then asking for his enabling grace to grow and change in the areas where the Spirit has convicted you. Many people find it helpful to write out their prayers. Space will be given for you to do this if you so desire.

Finally, take time to **share** what you are learning **with other believers.** Transparent, humble sharing helps cement truth in our hearts and mobilizes helpful accountability.

For Discussion:

1. Why is it so important that we have God's glory (both getting his glory and giving him glory) as our ultimate aim in Bible study?

2. As you work through this study in the months to come, what are some of the most important truths about God's attributes that you need to keep in mind?

3. The Bible is all about God! Not about us. While it is important that we keep God at the center of our Bible study, we also realize that Bible study does eventually come around to us. God intends it to be this way. He designed it so that when we behold his glory, it affects us. God's living and active Word changes us from one degree of glory to another. How do we keep this "all about God" and yet "also about us" perspective in balance?

4. Why is it crucial that we maintain a "gospel focus" as we seek to make personal application of Scripture to our lives?

God is Great

God is Sovereign

God rules over his creation.
He actively guides all events
to fulfill his purpose.

Job 42:2

I know that you can do all things,
and that no purpose of yours can be thwarted.

Prepare Your Heart

Prayer helps prepare our hearts to receive and respond to God's Word. Before beginning your study each day, humbly ask the Lord to open your eyes to his truth and to give you spiritual understanding.

"Please show me Your glory." (Exodus 33:18)

Memorize

❏ Take time each day to review both the attribute definition and corresponding verse, committing them to memory.

Meditate

❏ Spend a few minutes each day reading the verse in context and writing down the things the Lord shows you.[14] **(Observation)**

❏ Journal your answers to the meditation questions that are provided. **(Interpretation)**

❏ Add additional verses that you already know or discover on your own about this aspect of God's character.[15]

Apply

❏ Record specific actions steps you need to take in response to what God has shown you in his Word. **(Application)**

❏ Consider using *The Tree* diagram to "counsel yourself."

Share

❏ Take time to respond to God in prayer and praise.

❏ Share what you are learning with other believers.

---

[14] Use the basic elements of the inductive study method as a guide at whatever level you feel comfortable. But please remember that there is no "one right way" to study God's Word. God honors the one who is seeking him with a tender, humble heart.
[15] Cross references in the margin of your Bible or the concordance located in the back of your Bible can be helpful in finding other related Scripture passages.
.

Observation: What does God say about himself?

Context/Observations:
Consider the context of the verse and record what you learn. How is this verse/passage connected to what comes before and after it? Also write down any surface observations that jump out at you as you read through the passage.

_____

_____

_____

_____

_____

_____

_____

_____

_____

_____

_____

_____

_____

_____

_____

_____

_____

_____

_____

_____

_____

_____

Key words:
Use a word study tool to find out more about the meanings of key words (the Strong's number has been supplied).[16] Don't worry about finding something profound for every word; just try to discover the essential meaning of the main words in the passage.

I know = H3045 (verb)

_____

_____

_____

You can do = H3201 (verb)

_____

_____

_____

all things = H3605

_____

_____

_____

no = H3808

_____

_____

_____

purpose = H4209

_____

_____

_____

---

[16] It is best to look up word definitions in the original languages rather than English. There are many good online resources available to help with this process (such as blueletterbible.org)

of = H4480

_____

_____

_____

yours = H859

_____

_____

_____

can be thwarted = H1219 (verb)

_____

_____

_____

_____

Summarize the "Big Idea" of Job 42:2 in your own words:
Use the information you gathered in the observation section
to summarize the big idea of this verse. This will take some
time and thought, but it's worth the effort!

_____

_____

_____

_____

_____

_____

_____

_____

_____

_____

_____

Interpretation: What does it mean?

The goal of studying the Bible is understanding what God has communicated about himself so that we can know him and glorify him (Col. 1:9-10). Remember, the Bible is all about a Person! Review your notes from the observation section of your study as you seek to answer the following meditation questions. Journal your thoughts in the space provided.

❑ What specific truths do I learn about **God the Father**, **Jesus**, or the **Holy Spirit** from this passage?

_____

_____

_____

_____

_____

_____

_____

_____

_____

_____

_____

_____

_____

_____

_____

_____

_____

_____

_____

_____

❑ What does this passage teach me about man/myself?

_____

_____

_____

_____

_____

_____

_____

❑ Are there any promises to claim (stated or implied)? If so, list them below:

_____

_____

_____

_____

_____

_____

❑ Are there any commands to obey (stated or implied)? If so, list them below:

_____

_____

_____

_____

_____

❑ Use the space below to capture any other important truths the Lord taught you through your study:

_____

_____

_____

_____

_____

God's Sovereignty seen in Jesus: Identify at least one example of God's sovereignty attributed to Jesus or displayed in his earthly life.

_____

_____

_____

_____

_____

_____

Identify one **Bible example** of a person who demonstrated either belief or unbelief in God's sovereignty by their words and actions. Did this person give God glory or seek to rob God of his glory? What were the results (fruit) of their belief/ unbelief? Record your insights in the space below.

_____

_____

_____

_____

_____

_____

Additional Verses about God's Sovereignty:

Application: What should I do?

Prayerfully consider the specific action steps you need to take in response to what God has shown you in his Word. *What does it mean to live in the reality of God's sovereignty? Do you need to repent of rivaling God and seeking to steal his glory in any area of life? How can you become more effective in fulfilling your purpose to glorify him?* Use the prompts below to help you personalize what you are learning. Think about your relationship with God and your relationships with other people. Ask God to enable you to have a whole-hearted response to his Word (a "whole heart" includes your mind, desires, and will). Consider using *The Tree* diagram on the following page to "counsel yourself."

Think Bible!
Consider what you **believe**: All sin begins with a lie. During this study, what specific lies about God's sovereignty did you discover in your thinking?

_____

_____

_____

_____

How has meditating on God's sovereignty impacted or changed your **beliefs**?

_____

_____

_____

_____

Value Bible!
Consider what you **want**: How has meditating on God's sovereignty revealed misplaced **desires** or **affections**?

_____

_____

_____

_____

_____

Going forward, what steps can you take to better ground
your heart and mind in this truth about God? How will you
intentionally nurture a growing affection for what God loves
and values?

Live Bible!
"You don't really believe something until you believe it
enough to act on it." Obedience is expressed in and with
your body as you yield your will to God. Considering
your recent choices, how can you better respond to God's
sovereignty with trust, worship, and humble submission?

Consider your **actions**: What step(s) of obedience do you
need to take to demonstrate a yielded **will** to God?

_____

_____

_____

_____

_____

_____

In what practical ways does God want you to demonstrate
the reality of his sovereignty to those with whom you
interact (family, friends, co-workers, neighbors, etc.)?

_____

_____

_____

_____

_____

My Tree

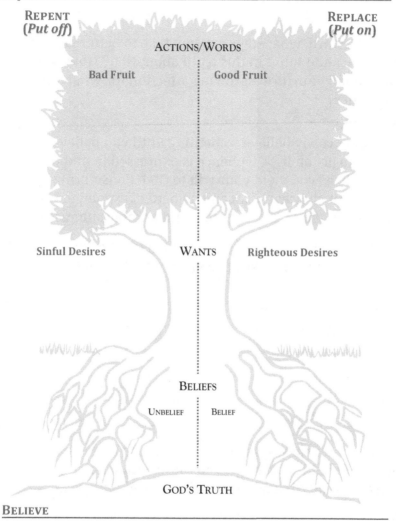

REPENT
(*Put off*)

REPLACE
(*Put on*)

ACTIONS/WORDS

Bad Fruit

Good Fruit

Sinful Desires

WANTS

Righteous Desires

BELIEFS

UNBELIEF

BELIEF

GOD'S TRUTH

BELIEVE

God says . . . I submit to it!

God is . . . I believe it!

Share

Share what you are learning with God through prayer. Although he already knows, it is good to take time to respond to him— praising him for who he is (God is always in control!) and asking for his enabling to grow in the areas where the Spirit has convicted you. Write out a simple prayer to God in the space below:

_____

_____

_____

_____

_____

_____

_____

_____

_____

_____

_____

_____

_____

_____

_____

_____

_____

_____

Finally, share what you are learning with other believers. Rejoice together in the truth about God! Encourage one another toward Christlikeness. Humbly open yourself up for accountability.

God is Sufficient

God is more than enough.
He alone satisfies

Acts 17:24-25

The God who made the world and everything in it, being Lord of heaven and earth, does not live in temples made by man, nor is he served by human hands, as though he needed anything, since he himself gives to all mankind life and breath and everything.

Prepare Your Heart

Prayer helps prepare our hearts to receive and respond to God's Word. Before beginning your study each day, humbly ask the Lord to open your eyes to his truth and to give you spiritual understanding.

"Please show me Your glory." (Exodus 33:18)

Memorize
❑ Take time each day to review both the attribute definition and corresponding verse, committing them to memory.

Meditate
❑ Spend a few minutes each day reading the verse in context and writing down the things the Lord shows you. **(Observation)**
❑ Journal your answers to the meditation questions that are provided. **(Interpretation)**
❑ Add additional verses that you already know or discover on your own about this aspect of God's character.

Apply
❑ Record specific actions steps you need to take in response to what God has shown you in his Word. **(Application)**
❑ Consider using *The Tree* diagram to "counsel yourself."

Share
❑ Take time to respond to God in prayer and praise.
❑ Share what you are learning with other believers.

Observation: What does God say about himself?

Context/Observations:
Consider the context of the verse and record what you learn. How is this verse/passage connected to what comes before and after it? Also write down any surface observations that jump out at you as you read through the passage.

_____
_____
_____
_____
_____
_____
_____
_____
_____
_____
_____
_____
_____
_____
_____
_____
_____
_____
_____
_____
_____
_____

Key words:
Use a word study tool to find out more about the meanings of key words (the Strong's number has been supplied). Don't worry about finding something profound for every word; just try to discover the essential meaning of the main words in the passage.

God = 2316

_____

_____

_____

who made = 4160 (verb)

_____

_____

_____

world = 2889

_____

_____

_____

everything = 3956

_____

_____

being = 5225 (verb)

_____

_____

Lord = 2962

_____

_____

_____

heaven = 3772

_____

_____

_____

earth = 1093

_____

_____

_____

not = 3756

_____

dwell = 2730 (verb)

_____

_____

_____

temples = 3485

_____

_____

_____

made by man = 5499

_____

_____

_____

nor = 3761

_____

is he served = 2323 (verb)

_____

_____

as though he needed = 4326 (verb)

anything = 5100

he himself = 846

gives = 1325 (verb)

all = 3956 (same as previous)
life = 2222

breath = 4157

everything = 3956 (same as previous)

Summarize the "Big Idea" of Acts 17:24-25 in your own words: Use the information you gathered in the observation section to summarize the big idea of this verse. This will take some time and thought, but it's worth the effort!

_____

_____

_____

_____

_____

_____

Interpretation: What does it mean?

The goal of studying the Bible is understanding what God has communicated about himself so that we can know him and glorify him (Col. 1:9-10). Remember, the Bible is all about a Person! Review your notes from the observation section of your study as you seek to answer the following meditation questions. Journal your thoughts in the space provided.

❑ What specific truths do I learn about **God the Father**, **Jesus**, or the **Holy Spirit** from this passage?

_____

_____

_____

_____

_____

_____

_____

_____

❏ What does this passage teach me about man/myself?

_____

_____

_____

_____

_____

_____

_____

❏ Are there any promises to claim (stated or implied)? If so, list them below:

_____

_____

_____

_____

_____

_____

❏ Are there any commands to obey (stated or implied)? If so, list them below:

_____

_____

_____

_____

_____

_____

❏ Use the space below to capture any other important truths the Lord taught you through your study:

_____

_____

_____

_____

_____

_____

God's Sufficiency seen in Jesus: Identify at least one example of God's sufficiency attributed to Jesus or displayed in his earthly life.

_____

_____

_____

_____

_____

_____

Identify one **Bible example** of a person who demonstrated either belief or unbelief in God's sufficiency by their words and actions. Did this person give God glory or seek to rob God of his glory? What were the results (fruit) of their belief/ unbelief? Record your insights in the space below.

_____

_____

_____

_____

_____

_____

Additional Verses about God's Sufficiency:

Application: What should I do?

Prayerfully consider the specific action steps you need to take in response to what God has shown you in his Word. *What does it mean to live in the reality of God's sufficiency? Do you need to repent of rivaling God and seeking to steal his glory in any area of life? How can you become more effective in fulfilling your purpose to glorify him?* Use the prompts below to help you personalize what you are learning. Think about your relationship with God and your relationships with other people. Ask God to enable you to have a **whole-hearted response** to his Word (a "whole heart" includes your mind, desires, and will). Consider using *The Tree* diagram on the following page to "counsel yourself."

Think Bible!
Consider what you **believe**: All sin begins with a lie. During this study, what specific lies about God's sufficiency did you discover in your thinking?

_____

_____

_____

_____

_____

_____

How has meditating on God's sufficiency impacted or changed your **beliefs**?

_____

_____

_____

_____

_____

_____

Value Bible!
Consider what you **want**: How has meditating on God's sufficiency revealed misplaced **desires** or **affections**?

_____

_____

_____

_____

_____

Going forward, what steps can you take to better ground your heart and mind in this truth about God? How will you intentionally nurture a growing affection for what God loves and values?

Live Bible!
"You don't really believe something until you believe it enough to act on it." Obedience is expressed in and with your body as you yield your will to God. Considering your recent choices, how can you better respond to God's sufficiency with trust, worship, and humble submission?

Consider your **actions**: What step(s) of obedience do you need to take to demonstrate a yielded **will** to God?

_____

_____

_____

_____

In what practical ways does God want you to demonstrate the reality of his sufficiency to those with whom you interact (family, friends, co-workers, neighbors, etc.)?

_____

_____

_____

_____

My Tree

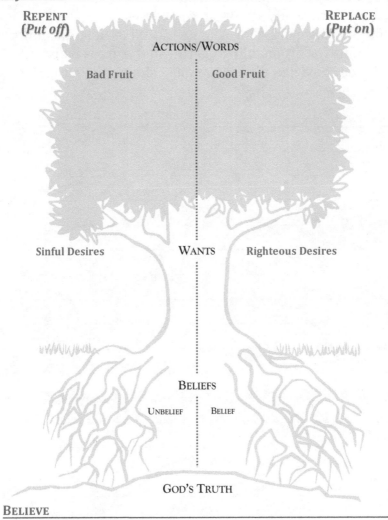

REPENT
(*Put off*)

REPLACE
(*Put on*)

ACTIONS/WORDS

Bad Fruit

Good Fruit

Sinful Desires

WANTS

Righteous Desires

BELIEFS

UNBELIEF

BELIEF

GOD'S TRUTH

BELIEVE

God says . . . I submit to it!

God is . . . I believe it!

Share

Share what you are learning with God through prayer. Although he already knows, it is good to take time to respond to him— praising him for who he is (God is all-sufficient!) and asking for his enabling to grow in the areas where the Spirit has convicted you. Write out a simple prayer to God in the space below:

_____

_____

_____

_____

_____

_____

_____

_____

_____

_____

_____

_____

_____

_____

_____

_____

_____

_____

_____

_____

Finally, share what you are learning with other believers. Rejoice together in the truth about God! Encourage one another toward Christlikeness. Humbly open yourself up for accountability.

God is All-Present

God is present everywhere
at all times.

Psalm 139:7–12

Where shall I go from your Spirit? Or where shall I flee from your presence? If I ascend to heaven, you are there! If I make my bed in Sheol, you are there! If I take the wings of the morning and dwell in the uttermost parts of the sea, even there your hand shall lead me, and your right hand shall hold me. If I say, "Surely the darkness shall cover me, and the light about me be night," even the darkness is not dark to you; the night is bright as the day, for darkness is as light with you.

Prepare Your Heart

Prayer helps prepare our hearts to receive and respond to God's Word. Before beginning your study each day, humbly ask the Lord to open your eyes to his truth and to give you spiritual understanding.

"Please show me Your glory." (Exodus 33:18)

Memorize

❏ Take time each day to review both the attribute definition and corresponding verse, committing them to memory.

Meditate

❏ Spend a few minutes each day reading the verse in context and writing down the things the Lord shows you. **(Observation)**

❏ Journal your answers to the meditation questions that are provided. **(Interpretation)**

❏ Add additional verses that you already know or discover on your own about this aspect of God's character.

Apply

❏ Record specific actions steps you need to take in response to what God has shown you in his Word. **(Application)**

❏ Consider using The Tree diagram to "counsel yourself."

Share

❏ Take time to respond to God in prayer and praise.

❏ Share what you are learning with other believers.

Observation: What does God say about Himself?

Context/Observations:
Consider the context of the verse and record what you learn. How is this verse/passage connected to what comes before and after it? Also write down any surface observations that jump out at you as you read through the passage.

_____

_____

_____

_____

_____

_____

_____

_____

_____

_____

_____

_____

_____

_____

_____

_____

_____

_____

_____

_____

_____

_____

Key words:
Use a word study tool to find out more about the meanings
of key words (the Strong's number has been supplied). Don't
worry about finding something profound for every word;
just try to discover the essential meaning of the main words
in the passage.

shall I go = H3212 (verb)

_____

_____

_____

from = H4480

_____

Spirit = H7307

_____

_____

can I flee = H1272 (verb)

_____

_____

presence = H6440

_____

_____

if = H518

_____

ascend = 5559 Aramaic/ H5266 Hebrew (verb)

_____

_____

_____

_____

heaven = H8064

_____

_____

make my bed in = H3331 (verb)

_____

_____

_____

Sheol = H7585

_____

_____

_____

you are there! = H2009

_____

_____

_____

take = H5375 (verb)

_____

the wings of = H3671

_____

_____

_____

the dawn = H7837

_____

_____

dwell = H7931 (verb)

_____

_____

uttermost = H319

_____

_____

even = H1571

_____

hand= H3027

_____

shall lead= H5148 (verb)

_____

right hand = H3225

_____

shall hold me = H270 (verb)

_____

surely = H389

_____

darkness = H2822

_____

cover = H7779 (verb)

_____

_____

light = H216

_____

_____

night = H3915

_____

even = H1571 (same as previous)
is (not) dark = H2821 (verb)

_____

is bright = H215 (verb)

_____

_____

day = H3117

_____

_____

Summarize the "Big Idea" of Psalm 139:7-12 in your own words: Use the information you gathered in the observation section to summarize the big idea of this verse. This will take some time and thought, but it's worth the effort!

_____

_____

_____

_____

_____

_____

_____

_____

Interpretation: What does it mean?

The goal of studying the Bible is understanding what God has communicated about Himself so that we can know him and glorify him (Col. 1:9-10). Remember, the Bible is all about a Person! Review your notes from the observation section of your study as you seek to answer the following meditation questions. Journal your thoughts in the space provided.

❏ What specific truths do I learn about **God the Father**, **Jesus**, or the **Holy Spirit** from this passage?

_____

_____

_____

_____

_____

_____

_____

_____

_____

❏ What does this passage teach me about man/myself?

_____

_____

_____

_____

_____

_____

_____

❑ Are there any promises to claim (stated or implied)? If so, list them below:

_____

_____

_____

_____

_____

_____

_____

❑ Are there any commands to obey (stated or implied)? If so, list them below:

_____

_____

_____

_____

_____

_____

_____

❑ Use the space below to capture any other important truths the Lord taught you through your study:

_____

_____

_____

_____

_____

_____

God's Omnipresence seen in Jesus: Identify at least one example of God's omnipresence attributed to Jesus or displayed in his earthly life.

_____

_____

_____

_____

_____

_____

_____

_____

_____

_____

Identify one **Bible example** of a person who demonstrated either belief or unbelief in God's omnipresence by their words and actions. Did this person give God glory or seek to rob God of his glory? What were the results (fruit) of their belief/unbelief? Record your insights in the space below.

_____

_____

_____

_____

_____

_____

_____

_____

_____

_____

Additional Verses about God's Omnipresence:

Application: What should I do?

Prayerfully consider the specific action steps you need to take in response to what God has shown you in his Word. *What does it mean to live in the reality of God's omnipresence? Do you need to repent of rivaling God and seeking to steal his glory in any area of life? How can you become more effective in fulfilling your purpose to glorify him?* Use the prompts below to help you personalize what you are learning. Think about your relationship with God and your relationships with other people. Ask God to enable you to have a **whole-hearted response** to his Word (a "whole heart" includes your mind, desires, and will). Consider using *The Tree* diagram on the following page to "counsel yourself."

Think Bible!
Consider what you **believe**: All sin begins with a lie. During this study, what specific lies about God's omnipresence did you discover in your thinking?

_____

_____

_____

_____

_____

How has meditating on God's omnipresence impacted or changed your **beliefs**?

_____

_____

_____

_____

_____

Value Bible!
Consider what you **want**: How has meditating on God's omnipresence revealed misplaced **desires** or **affections**?

_____

_____

_____

_____

_____

Going forward, what steps can you take to better ground your heart and mind in this truth about God? How will you intentionally nurture a growing affection for what God loves and values?

Live Bible!
"You don't really believe something until you believe it enough to act on it." Obedience is expressed in and with your body as you yield your will to God. Considering your recent choices, how can you better respond to God's omnipresence with trust, worship, and humble submission?

Consider your **actions**: What step(s) of obedience do you need to take to demonstrate a yielded **will** to God?

_____

_____

_____

_____

In what practical ways does God want you to demonstrate the reality of his omnipresence to those with whom you interact (family, friends, co-workers, neighbors, etc.)?

_____

_____

_____

_____

My Tree

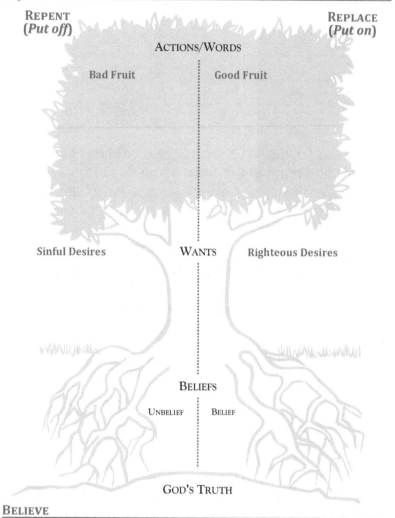

REPENT
(*Put off*)

REPLACE
(*Put on*)

ACTIONS/WORDS

Bad Fruit

Good Fruit

Sinful Desires

WANTS

Righteous Desires

BELIEFS

UNBELIEF

BELIEF

GOD'S TRUTH

BELIEVE

God says . . . I submit to it!

God is . . . I believe it!

Share

Share what you are learning with God through prayer.
Although he already knows, it is good to take time to respond
to him— praising him for who he is (God is always present!)
and asking for his enabling to grow in the areas where the
Spirit has convicted you. Write out a simple prayer to God in
the space below:

_____

_____

_____

_____

_____

_____

_____

_____

_____

_____

_____

_____

_____

_____

_____

_____

_____

_____

Finally, share what you are learning with other believers.
Rejoice together in the truth about God! Encourage one
another toward Christlikeness. Humbly open yourself up for
accountability.

God is Immutable

God's nature is absolutely unchangeable.
He cannot change because he is perfect.
He is always the same.

Hebrews 1:10-12

And, "You, Lord, laid the foundation of the earth in the beginning, and the heavens are the work of your hands; they will perish, but you remain; they will all wear out like a garment, like a robe you will roll them up, like a garment they will be changed. But you are the same, and your years will have no end."

Prepare Your Heart

Prayer helps prepare our hearts to receive and respond to God's Word. Before beginning your study each day, humbly ask the Lord to open your eyes to his truth and to give you spiritual understanding.

"Please show me Your glory." (Exodus 33:18)

Memorize

❑ Take time each day to review both the attribute definition and corresponding verse, committing them to memory.

Meditate

❑ Spend a few minutes each day reading the verse in context and writing down the things the Lord shows you. **(Observation)**

❑ Journal your answers to the meditation questions that are provided. **(Interpretation)**

❑ Add additional verses that you already know or discover on your own about this aspect of God's character.

Apply

❑ Record specific actions steps you need to take in response to what God has shown you in his Word. **(Application)**

❑ Consider using *The Tree* diagram to "counsel yourself."

Share

❑ Take time to respond to God in prayer and praise.

❑ Share what you are learning with other believers.

Observation: What does God say about Himself?

Context/Observations:
Consider the context of the verse and record what you learn.
How is this verse/passage connected to what comes before
and after it? Also write down any surface observations that
jump out at you as you read through the passage.

_____

_____

_____

_____

_____

_____

_____

_____

_____

_____

_____

_____

_____

_____

_____

_____

_____

_____

_____

_____

_____

_____

Key words:
Use a word study tool to find out more about the meanings of key words (the Strong's number has been supplied). Don't worry about finding something profound for every word; just try to discover the essential meaning of the main words in the passage.

Lord = 2962

_____

_____

_____

laid the foundation of = 2311 (verb)

_____

_____

_____

earth = 1093

_____

in the beginning = 746

_____

_____

heavens = 3772

_____

the work = 2041

_____

_____

_____

hands = 5495

_____

_____

will perish = 622 (verb)

_____

_____

but = 1161

_____

remain = 1265 (verb)

_____

_____

will wear out = 3822 (verb)

_____

_____

_____

like = 5613

_____

garment = 2440

_____

robe = 4018

_____

will roll up = 1507 (verb)

_____

_____

_____

be changed = 236 (verb)

_____

_____

_____

but = 1161 (same as previous)

are = 1510 (verb)

_____

_____

the same = 846

_____

_____

years = 2094

_____

_____

no = 3756

_____

will have end = 1587 (verb)

_____

_____

_____

_____

Summarize the "Big Idea" of Hebrews 1:10-12 in your own words: Use the information you gathered in the observation section to summarize the big idea of this verse. This will take some time and thought, but it's worth the effort!

_____

_____

_____

_____

_____

_____

Interpretation: What does it mean?

The goal of studying the Bible is understanding what God has communicated about Himself so that we can know him and glorify him (Col. 1:9-10). Remember, the Bible is all about a Person! Review your notes from the observation section of your study as you seek to answer the following meditation questions. Journal your thoughts in the space provided.

❑ What specific truths do I learn about **God the Father**, **Jesus**, or the **Holy Spirit** from this passage?

_____

_____

_____

_____

_____

_____

_____

_____

_____

❑ What does this passage teach me about man/myself?

_____

_____

_____

_____

_____

_____

_____

_____

❑ Are there any promises to claim (stated or implied)? If so, list them below:

_____

_____

_____

_____

_____

_____

_____

❑ Are there any commands to obey (stated or implied)? If so, list them below:

_____

_____

_____

_____

_____

_____

_____

❑ Use the space below to capture any other important truths the Lord taught you through your study:

_____

_____

_____

_____

_____

_____

God's Immutability seen in Jesus: Identify at least one example of God's immutability attributed to Jesus or displayed in his earthly life.

_____

_____

_____

_____

_____

_____

_____

_____

_____

_____

Identify one **Bible example** of a person who demonstrated either belief or unbelief in God's immutability by their words and actions. Did this person give God glory or seek to rob God of his glory? What were the results (fruit) of their belief/unbelief? Record your insights in the space below.

_____

_____

_____

_____

_____

_____

_____

_____

_____

_____

Additional Verses about God's Immutability:

Application: What should I do?

Prayerfully consider the specific action steps you need to take in response to what God has shown you in his Word. *What does it mean to live in the reality of God's immutability? Do you need to repent of rivaling God and seeking to steal his glory in any area of life? How can you become more effective in fulfilling your purpose to glorify him?* Use the prompts below to help you personalize what you are learning. Think about your relationship with God and your relationships with other people. Ask God to enable you to have a **whole-hearted response** to his Word (a "whole heart" includes your mind, desires, and will). Consider using *The Tree* diagram on the following page to "counsel yourself."

Think Bible!
Consider what you **believe**: All sin begins with a lie. During this study, what specific lies about God's immutability did you discover in your thinking?

_____

_____

_____

_____

_____

_____

How has meditating on God's immutability impacted or changed your **beliefs**?

_____

_____

_____

_____

_____

_____

Value Bible!
Consider what you **want**: How has meditating on God's immutability revealed misplaced **desires** or **affections**?

_____

_____

_____

_____

_____

Going forward, what steps can you take to better ground your heart and mind in this truth about God? How will you intentionally nurture a growing affection for what God loves and values?

Live Bible!
"You don't really believe something until you believe it enough to act on it." Obedience is expressed in and with your body as you yield your will to God. Considering your recent choices, how can you better respond to God's immutability with trust, worship, and humble submission?

Consider your **actions**: What step(s) of obedience do you need to take to demonstrate a yielded **will** to God?

_____

_____

_____

_____

In what practical ways does God want you to demonstrate the reality of his immutability to those with whom you interact (family, friends, co-workers, neighbors, etc.)?

_____

_____

_____

_____

My Tree

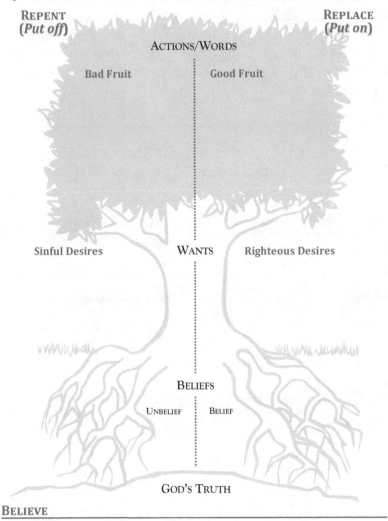

REPENT
(*Put off*)

REPLACE
(*Put on*)

ACTIONS/WORDS

Bad Fruit

Good Fruit

Sinful Desires

WANTS

Righteous Desires

BELIEFS

UNBELIEF

BELIEF

GOD'S TRUTH

BELIEVE

God says . . . I submit to it!

God is . . . I believe it!

Share

Share what you are learning with God through prayer. Although he already knows, it is good to take time to respond to him— praising him for who he is (God *never* changes!) and asking for his enabling to grow in the areas where the Spirit has convicted you. Write out a simple prayer to God in the space below:

_____

_____

_____

_____

_____

_____

_____

_____

_____

_____

_____

_____

_____

_____

_____

_____

_____

_____

Finally, share what you are learning with other believers. Rejoice together in the truth about God! Encourage one another toward Christlikeness. Humbly open yourself up for accountability.

God is Good

God is Wisdom

God always chooses the best goals
and the best ways to reach those goals.

Daniel 2:20-22

Daniel answered and said: "Blessed be the name of God forever and ever, to whom belong wisdom and might. He changes times and seasons; he removes kings and sets up kings; he gives wisdom to the wise and knowledge to those who have understanding; he reveals deep and hidden things; he knows what is in the darkness, and the light dwells with him."

Prepare Your Heart

Prayer helps prepare our hearts to receive and respond to God's Word. Before beginning your study each day, humbly ask the Lord to open your eyes to his truth and to give you spiritual understanding.

"Please show me Your glory." (Exodus 33:18)

Memorize
❑ Take time each day to review both the attribute definition and corresponding verse, committing them to memory.

Meditate
❑ Spend a few minutes each day reading the verse in context and writing down the things the Lord shows you. **(Observation)**
❑ Journal your answers to the meditation questions that are provided. **(Interpretation)**
❑ Add additional verses that you already know or discover on your own about this aspect of God's character.

Apply
❑ Record specific actions steps you need to take in response to what God has shown you in his Word. **(Application)**
❑ Consider using *The Tree* diagram to "counsel yourself."

Share
❑ Take time to respond to God in prayer and praise.
❑ Share what you are learning with other believers.

Observation: What does God say about Himself?

Context/Observations:
Consider the context of the verse and record what you learn.
How is this verse/passage connected to what comes before
and after it? Also write down any surface observations that
jump out at you as you read through the passage.

_____
_____
_____
_____
_____
_____
_____
_____
_____
_____
_____
_____
_____
_____
_____
_____
_____
_____
_____
_____
_____
_____
_____

Key words:

Use a word study tool to find out more about the meanings of key words (the Strong's number has been supplied).[17] Don't worry about finding something profound for every word; just try to discover the essential meaning of the main words in the passage.

blessed = H1289

_____

_____

_____

be = H1934 (verb)

_____

the name = H8036

_____

God = H426

_____

forever and ever = H5957

_____

_____

wisdom = H2452

_____

_____

_____

---

[17] Due to the original audience, this section of the book of Daniel was originally written in Aramaic. If you are using an online word study tool to research the Strong's number, you may notice a corresponding Hebrew word which will give you further insight into word meaning.

might = H1370

---

changes = H8133 (verb)

---

times = H5732

---

seasons = H2166

---

removes = H5709 (verb)

---

kings = H4430

---

sets up = H6966 (verb)

---

gives = H3052 (verb)

---

wise = H2445

_____

_____

_____

knowledge = H4486

_____

_____

_____

understanding = H999

_____

_____

_____

reveals = H1541 (verb)

_____

_____

deep = H5994

_____

_____

_____

hidden things = H5642

_____

_____

_____

knows = H3046 (verb)

_____

_____

_____

the darkness = H2816

_____

the light = H5094

_____

_____

_____

dwells = H8271 (verb)

_____

_____

_____

Summarize the "Big Idea" of Daniel 2:20-22 in your own words: Use the information you gathered in the observation section to summarize the big idea of this verse. This will take some time and thought, but it's worth the effort!

_____

_____

_____

_____

_____

_____

_____

_____

_____

_____

_____

_____

_____

Interpretation: What does it mean?

The goal of studying the Bible is understanding what God has communicated about himself so that we can know him and glorify him (Col. 1:9-10). Remember, the Bible is all about a Person! Review your notes from the observation section of your study as you seek to answer the following meditation questions. Journal your thoughts in the space provided.

❑ What specific truths do I learn about **God the Father**, **Jesus**, or the **Holy Spirit** from this passage?

_____

_____

_____

_____

_____

_____

_____

_____

_____

❑ What does this passage teach me about man/myself?

_____

_____

_____

_____

_____

_____

_____

❑ Are there any promises to claim (stated or implied)? If so, list them below:

_____

_____

_____

_____

_____

_____

_____

❑ Are there any commands to obey (stated or implied)? If so, list them below:

_____

_____

_____

_____

_____

_____

_____

❑ Use the space below to capture any other important truths the Lord taught you through your study:

_____

_____

_____

_____

_____

_____

God's wisdom seen in Jesus: Identify at least one example of God's wisdom attributed to Jesus or displayed in his earthly life.

_____

_____

_____

_____

_____

_____

_____

_____

_____

_____

Identify one **Bible example** of a person who demonstrated either belief or unbelief in God's wisdom by their words and actions. Did this person give God glory or seek to rob God of his glory? What were the results (fruit) of their belief/ unbelief? Record your insights in the space below.

_____

_____

_____

_____

_____

_____

_____

_____

_____

_____

Additional Verses about God's Wisdom:

Application: What should I do?

Prayerfully consider the specific action steps you need to take in response to what God has shown you in his Word. *What does it mean to live in the reality of God's wisdom? Do you need to repent of rivaling God and seeking to steal his glory in any area of life? How can you become more effective in fulfilling your purpose to glorify him?* Use the prompts below to help you personalize what you are learning. Think about your relationship with God and your relationships with other people. Ask God to enable you to have a **whole-hearted response** to his Word (a "whole heart" includes your mind, desires, and will). Consider using *The Tree* diagram on the following page to "counsel yourself."

Think Bible!
Consider what you **believe**: All sin begins with a lie. During this study, what specific lies about God's wisdom did you discover in your thinking?

_____

_____

_____

_____

_____

How has meditating on God's wisdom impacted or changed your **beliefs**?

_____

_____

_____

_____

_____

Value Bible!
Consider what you **want**: How has meditating on God's wisdom revealed misplaced **desires** or **affections**?

_____

_____

_____

_____

_____

Going forward, what steps can you take to better ground your heart and mind in this truth about God? How will you intentionally nurture a growing affection for what God loves and values?

Live Bible!
"You don't really believe something until you believe it enough to act on it." Obedience is expressed in and with your body as you yield your will to God. Considering your recent choices, how can you better respond to God's wisdom with trust, worship, and humble submission?

Consider your **actions**: What step(s) of obedience do you need to take to demonstrate a yielded **will** to God?

_____

_____

_____

_____

In what practical ways does God want you to demonstrate the reality of his wisdom to those with whom you interact (family, friends, co-workers, neighbors, etc.)?

_____

_____

_____

_____

My Tree

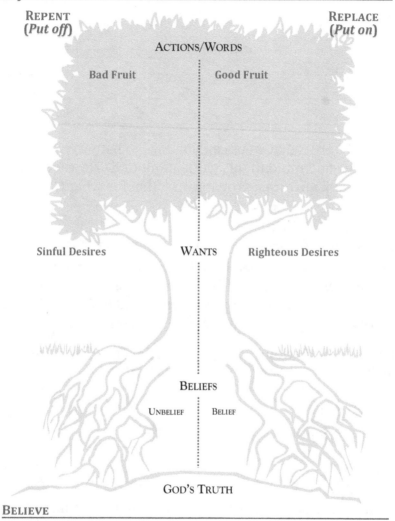

REPENT
(*Put off*)

REPLACE
(*Put on*)

ACTIONS/WORDS

Bad Fruit

Good Fruit

Sinful Desires

WANTS

Righteous Desires

BELIEFS

UNBELIEF

BELIEF

GOD'S TRUTH

BELIEVE

God says . . . I submit to it!

God is . . . I believe it!

Share

Share what you are learning with God through prayer. Although he already knows, it is good to take time to respond to him— praising him for who he is (God is *always* wise!) and asking for his enabling to grow in the areas where the Spirit has convicted you. Write out a simple prayer to God in the space below:

_____

_____

_____

_____

_____

_____

_____

_____

_____

_____

_____

_____

_____

_____

_____

_____

_____

_____

Finally, share what you are learning with other believers. Rejoice together in the truth about God! Encourage one another toward Christlikeness. Humbly open yourself up for accountability.

God is Peace

God is separate from all
confusion and disorder.

2 Thessalonians 3:16

*Now may the Lord of peace himself give you peace
at all times in every way. The Lord be with you all.*

Prepare Your Heart

Prayer helps prepare our hearts to receive and respond to God's Word. Before beginning your study each day, humbly ask the Lord to open your eyes to his truth and to give you spiritual understanding.

"Please show me Your glory." (Exodus 33:18)

Memorize
❏ Take time each day to review both the attribute definition and corresponding verse, committing them to memory.

Meditate
❏ Spend a few minutes each day reading the verse in context and writing down the things the Lord shows you. **(Observation)**
❏ Journal your answers to the meditation questions that are provided. **(Interpretation)**
❏ Add additional verses that you already know or discover on your own about this aspect of God's character.

Apply
❏ Record specific actions steps you need to take in response to what God has shown you in his Word. **(Application)**
❏ Consider using *The Tree* diagram to "counsel yourself."

Share
❏ Take time to respond to God in prayer and praise.
❏ Share what you are learning with other believers.

Observation: What does God say about Himself?

Context/Observations:
Consider the context of the verse and record what you learn.
How is this verse/passage connected to what comes before
and after it? Also write down any surface observations that
jump out at you as you read through the passage.

_____
_____
_____
_____
_____
_____
_____
_____
_____
_____
_____
_____
_____
_____
_____
_____
_____
_____
_____
_____
_____
_____
_____
_____

Key words:
Use a word study tool to find out more about the meanings
of key words (the Strong's number has been supplied). Don't
worry about finding something profound for every word;
just try to discover the essential meaning of the main words
in the passage.

Lord = 2962

_____

_____

_____

peace = 1515

_____

_____

_____

_____

give = 1325 (verb)

_____

_____

_____

_____

peace = 1515 (same as previous)
all = 3956

_____

times = 1223

_____

_____

_____

every = 3956 (same as previous)

way = 5158

_____

_____

_____

_____

Lord = 2962 (same as previous)

be with = 3326

_____

_____

_____

all = 3956 (same as previous)

Summarize the "Big Idea" of 2 Thessalonians 3:16 in your own words: Use the information you gathered in the observation section to summarize the big idea of this verse. This will take some time and thought, but it's worth the effort!

_____

_____

_____

_____

_____

_____

_____

_____

_____

_____

_____

_____

Interpretation: What does it mean?

The goal of studying the Bible is understanding what God has communicated about Himself so that we can know him and glorify him (Col. 1:9-10). Remember, the Bible is all about a Person! Review your notes from the observation section of your study as you seek to answer the following meditation questions. Journal your thoughts in the space provided.

❑ What specific truths do I learn about **God the Father**, **Jesus**, or the **Holy Spirit** from this passage?

_____

_____

_____

_____

_____

_____

_____

_____

_____

❑ What does this passage teach me about man/myself?

_____

_____

_____

_____

_____

_____

_____

_____

❑ Are there any promises to claim (stated or implied)? If so, list them below:

_____

_____

_____

_____

_____

_____

_____

❑ Are there any commands to obey (stated or implied)? If so, list them below:

_____

_____

_____

_____

_____

_____

_____

❑ Use the space below to capture any other important truths the Lord taught you through your study:

_____

_____

_____

_____

_____

_____

God's peace seen in Jesus: Identify at least one example of God's peace attributed to Jesus or displayed in his earthly life.

_____

_____

_____

_____

_____

_____

_____

_____

_____

_____

Identify one **Bible example** of a person who demonstrated either belief or unbelief in God's peace by their words and actions. Did this person give God glory or seek to rob God of his glory? What were the results (fruit) of their belief/ unbelief? Record your insights in the space below.

_____

_____

_____

_____

_____

_____

_____

_____

_____

_____

Additional Verses about God's Peace:

Application: What should I do?

Prayerfully consider the specific action steps you need to take in response to what God has shown you in his Word. *What does it mean to live in the reality of God's peace? Do you need to repent of rivaling God and seeking to steal his glory in any area of life? How can you become more effective in fulfilling your purpose to glorify him?* Use the prompts below to help you personalize what you are learning. Think about your relationship with God and your relationships with other people. Ask God to enable you to have a **whole-hearted response** to his Word (a "whole heart" includes your mind, desires, and will). Consider using *The Tree* diagram on the following page to "counsel yourself."

Think Bible!
Consider what you **believe**: All sin begins with a lie. During this study, what specific lies about God's peace did you discover in your thinking?

_____

_____

_____

_____

_____

How has meditating on God's peace impacted or changed your **beliefs**?

_____

_____

_____

_____

_____

Value Bible!
Consider what you **want**: How has meditating on God's peace revealed misplaced **desires** or **affections**?

_____

_____

_____

_____

_____

Going forward, what steps can you take to better ground your heart and mind in this truth about God? How will you intentionally nurture a growing affection for what God loves and values?

Live Bible!
"You don't really believe something until you believe it enough to act on it." Obedience is expressed in and with your body as you yield your will to God. Considering your recent choices, how can you better respond to God's peace with trust, worship, and humble submission?

Consider your **actions**: What step(s) of obedience do you need to take to demonstrate a yielded **will** to God?

_____

_____

_____

_____

In what practical ways does God want you to demonstrate the reality of his peace to those with whom you interact (family, friends, co-workers, neighbors, etc.)?

_____

_____

_____

_____

My Tree

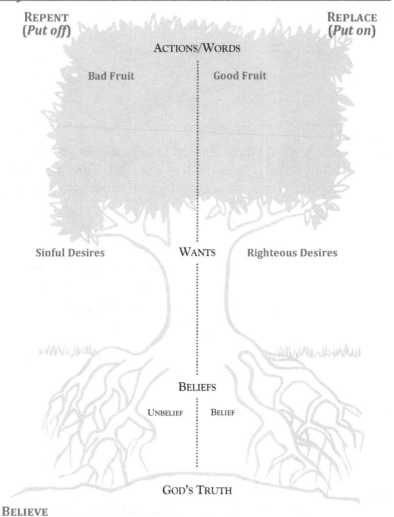

REPENT
(*Put off*)

REPLACE
(*Put on*)

ACTIONS/WORDS

Bad Fruit   Good Fruit

Sinful Desires   WANTS   Righteous Desires

BELIEFS

UNBELIEF   BELIEF

GOD'S TRUTH

BELIEVE

God says . . . I submit to it!

God is . . . I believe it!

Share

Share what you are learning with God through prayer. Although he already knows, it is good to take time to respond to him— praising him for who he is (God is *always* the Lord of peace!) and asking for his enabling to grow in the areas where the Spirit has convicted you. Write out a simple prayer to God in the space below:

_____

_____

_____

_____

_____

_____

_____

_____

_____

_____

_____

_____

_____

_____

_____

_____

_____

_____

Finally, share what you are learning with other believers. Rejoice together in the truth about God! Encourage one another toward Christlikeness. Humbly open yourself up for accountability.

God is Just

God is the final standard of what is right.
He will always punish the wicked and reward
the righteous without favoritism.

Deuteronomy 32:4

The Rock, his work is perfect, for all his ways are justice.
A God of faithfulness and without iniquity,
just and upright is he.

Prepare Your Heart

Prayer helps prepare our hearts to receive and respond to God's Word. Before beginning your study each day, humbly ask the Lord to open your eyes to his truth and to give you spiritual understanding.

"Please show me Your glory." (Exodus 33:18)

Memorize
- [ ] Take time each day to review both the attribute definition and corresponding verse, committing them to memory.

Meditate
- [ ] Spend a few minutes each day reading the verse in context and writing down the things the Lord shows you. **(Observation)**
- [ ] Journal your answers to the meditation questions that are provided. **(Interpretation)**
- [ ] Add additional verses that you already know or discover on your own about this aspect of God's character.

Apply
- [ ] Record specific actions steps you need to take in response to what God has shown you in his Word. **(Application)**
- [ ] Consider using *The Tree* diagram to "counsel yourself."

Share
- [ ] Take time to respond to God in prayer and praise.
- [ ] Share what you are learning with other believers.

Observation: What does God say about Himself?

Context/Observations:
Consider the context of the verse and record what you learn. How is this verse/passage connected to what comes before and after it? Also write down any surface observations that jump out at you as you read through the passage.

_____
_____
_____
_____
_____
_____
_____
_____
_____
_____
_____
_____
_____
_____
_____
_____
_____
_____
_____
_____
_____
_____
_____
_____

Key words:

Use a word study tool to find out more about the meanings of key words (the Strong's number has been supplied). Don't worry about finding something profound for every word; just try to discover the essential meaning of the main words in the passage.

The Rock = H6697

_____

_____

_____

work = H6467

_____

_____

_____

is perfect = H8549

_____

_____

_____

all = H3605

_____

ways = H1870

_____

_____

_____

are justice = H4941

_____

_____

_____

a God of = H410

_____

_____

_____

faithfulness = H530

_____

_____

_____

without = H369

_____

_____

iniquity = H5766

_____

_____

_____

just = H6662

_____

_____

_____

upright = H3477

_____

_____

_____

Summarize the "Big Idea" of Deuteronomy 32:4 in your own words: Use the information you gathered in the observation section to summarize the big idea of this verse. This will take some time and thought, but it's worth the effort!

_____

_____

_____

_____

_____

_____

_____

Interpretation: What does it mean?

The goal of studying the Bible is understanding what God has communicated about Himself so that we can know him and glorify him (Col. 1:9-10). Remember, the Bible is all about a Person! Review your notes from the observation section of your study as you seek to answer the following meditation questions. Journal your thoughts in the space provided.

❑ What specific truths do I learn about **God the Father**, **Jesus**, or the **Holy Spirit** from this passage?

_____

_____

_____

_____

_____

_____

_____

_____

❑ What does this passage teach me about man/myself?

_____

_____

_____

_____

_____

_____

_____

_____

❑ Are there any promises to claim (stated or implied)? If so, list them below:

_____

_____

_____

_____

_____

_____

_____

❑ Are there any commands to obey (stated or implied)? If so, list them below:

_____

_____

_____

_____

_____

_____

_____

❑ Use the space below to capture any other important truths the Lord taught you through your study:

_____

_____

_____

_____

_____

_____

_____

_____

_____

God's justice seen in Jesus: Identify at least one example of God's justice attributed to Jesus or displayed in his earthly life.

_____

_____

_____

_____

_____

_____

_____

_____

_____

_____

_____

_____

_____

_____

Identify one **Bible example** of a person who demonstrated either belief or unbelief in God's justice by their words and actions. Did this person give God glory or seek to rob God of his glory? What were the results (fruit) of their belief/ unbelief? Record your insights in the space below.

_____

_____

_____

_____

_____

_____

_____

_____

_____

_____

Additional Verses about God's Justice:

Application: What should I do?

Prayerfully consider the specific action steps you need to take in response to what God has shown you in his Word. *What does it mean to live in the reality of God's justice? Do you need to repent of rivaling God and seeking to steal his glory in any area of life? How can you become more effective in fulfilling your purpose to glorify him?* Use the prompts below to help you personalize what you are learning. Think about your relationship with God and your relationships with other people. Ask God to enable you to have a **whole-hearted response** to his Word (a "whole heart" includes your mind, desires, and will). Consider using *The Tree* diagram on the following page to "counsel yourself."

Think Bible!
Consider what you **believe**: All sin begins with a lie. During this study, what specific lies about God's justice did you discover in your thinking?

_____

_____

_____

_____

_____

_____

How has meditating on God's justice impacted or changed your **beliefs**?

_____

_____

_____

_____

_____

_____

Value Bible!
Consider what you **want**: How has meditating on God's justice revealed misplaced **desires** or **affections**?

_____

_____

_____

_____

_____

Going forward, what steps can you take to better ground your heart and mind in this truth about God? How will you intentionally nurture a growing affection for what God loves and values?

Live Bible!
"You don't really believe something until you believe it enough to act on it." Obedience is expressed in and with your body as you yield your will to God. Considering your recent choices, how can you better respond to God's justice with trust, worship, and humble submission?

Consider your **actions**: What step(s) of obedience do you need to take to demonstrate a yielded **will** to God?

_____

_____

_____

_____

In what practical ways does God want you to demonstrate the reality of his justice to those with whom you interact (family, friends, co-workers, neighbors, etc.)?

_____

_____

_____

_____

My Tree

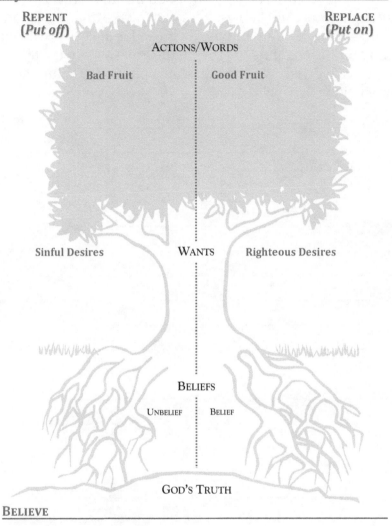

REPENT
(*Put off*)

REPLACE
(*Put on*)

ACTIONS/WORDS

Bad Fruit

Good Fruit

Sinful Desires

WANTS

Righteous Desires

BELIEFS

UNBELIEF

BELIEF

GOD'S TRUTH

BELIEVE

God says . . . I submit to it!

God is . . . I believe it!

Share

Share what you are learning with God through prayer. Although he already knows, it is good to take time to respond to him— praising him for who he is (God is *always* just!) and asking for his enabling to grow in the areas where the Spirit has convicted you. Write out a simple prayer to God in the space below:

_____

_____

_____

_____

_____

_____

_____

_____

_____

_____

_____

_____

_____

_____

_____

_____

Finally, share what you are learning with other believers. Rejoice together in the truth about God! Encourage one another toward Christlikeness. Humbly open yourself up for accountability.

God is Merciful

God is slow to anger, not giving us
the punishment that we deserve.

Luke 6:35-36

*But love your enemies, and do good, and lend,
expecting nothing in return, and your reward
will be great, and you will be sons of the Most High,
for he is kind to the ungrateful and the evil.
Be merciful, even as your Father is merciful.*

Prepare Your Heart

Prayer helps prepare our hearts to receive and respond to God's Word. Before beginning your study each day, humbly ask the Lord to open your eyes to his truth and to give you spiritual understanding.

"Please show me Your glory." (Exodus 33:18)

Memorize
❏ Take time each day to review both the attribute definition and corresponding verse, committing them to memory.

Meditate
❏ Spend a few minutes each day reading the verse in context and writing down the things the Lord shows you. **(Observation)**
❏ Journal your answers to the meditation questions that are provided. **(Interpretation)**
❏ Add additional verses that you already know or discover on your own about this aspect of God's character.

Apply
❏ Record specific actions steps you need to take in response to what God has shown you in his Word. **(Application)**
❏ Consider using *The Tree* diagram to "counsel yourself."

Share
❏ Take time to respond to God in prayer and praise.
❏ Share what you are learning with other believers.

Observation: What does God say about Himself?

Context/Observations:
Consider the context of the verse and record what you learn. How is this verse/passage connected to what comes before and after it? Also write down any surface observations that jump out at you as you read through the passage.

_____

_____

_____

_____

_____

_____

_____

_____

_____

_____

_____

_____

_____

_____

_____

_____

_____

_____

_____

_____

_____

_____

_____

Key words:
Use a word study tool to find out more about the meanings of key words (the Strong's number has been supplied). Don't worry about finding something profound for every word; just try to discover the essential meaning of the main words in the passage.

but = 4133

_____

love = 25 (verb)

_____

_____

_____

enemies = 2190

_____

_____

_____

do good = 15 (verb)

_____

_____

_____

lend = 1155 (verb)

_____

_____

_____

expecting in return = 560 (verb)

_____

_____

_____

nothing = 3367

_____

_____

reward = 3408

_____

_____

_____

will be = **1510** (verb, future middle indicative)

_____

_____

_____

great = 4183

_____

_____

_____

will be = **1510** (same as previous)
sons = 5207

_____

_____

_____

of the Most High = 5310

_____

_____

_____

for = 3754

_____

_____

is = 1510 (verb, present active indicative)

___

kind = 5543

___

___

___

ungrateful = 884

___

___

___

evil = 4190

___

___

___

be = 1096 (verb)

___

merciful = 3629

___

___

___

even as = 2531

___

Father = 3962

___

___

merciful = 3629 (same as previous)

Summarize the "Big Idea" of Luke 6:35-36 in your own words: Use the information you gathered in the observation section to summarize the big idea of this verse. This will take some time and thought, but it's worth the effort!

_____

_____

_____

_____

_____

_____

Interpretation: What does it mean?

The goal of studying the Bible is understanding what God has communicated about Himself so that we can know him and glorify him (Col. 1:9-10). Remember, the Bible is all about a Person! Review your notes from the observation section of your study as you seek to answer the following meditation questions. Journal your thoughts in the space provided.

❑ What specific truths do I learn about **God the Father**, **Jesus**, or the **Holy Spirit** from this passage?

_____

_____

_____

_____

_____

_____

_____

_____

❑ What does this passage teach me about man/myself?

_____

_____

_____

_____

_____

_____

_____

❑ Are there any promises to claim (stated or implied)? If so, list them below:

_____

_____

_____

_____

_____

_____

❑ Are there any commands to obey (stated or implied)? If so, list them below:

_____

_____

_____

_____

_____

_____

❑ Use the space below to capture any other important truths the Lord taught you through your study:

_____

_____

_____

_____

_____

_____

_____

_____

_____

God's mercy seen in Jesus: Identify at least one example of God's mercy attributed to Jesus or displayed in his earthly life.

_____

_____

_____

_____

_____

_____

_____

_____

_____

_____

_____

_____

_____

Identify one **Bible example** of a person who demonstrated either belief or unbelief in God's mercy by their words and actions. Did this person give God glory or seek to rob God of his glory? What were the results (fruit) of their belief/ unbelief? Record your insights in the space below.

_____

_____

_____

_____

_____

_____

_____

_____

_____

_____

Additional Verses about God's Mercy:

Application: What should I do?

Prayerfully consider the specific action steps you need to take in response to what God has shown you in his Word. *What does it mean to live in the reality of God's mercy? Do you need to repent of rivaling God and seeking to steal his glory in any area of life? How can you become more effective in fulfilling your purpose to glorify him?* Use the prompts below to help you personalize what you are learning. Think about your relationship with God and your relationships with other people. Ask God to enable you to have a **whole-hearted response** to his Word (a "whole heart" includes your mind, desires, and will). Consider using *The Tree* diagram on the following page to "counsel yourself."

Think Bible!
Consider what you **believe**: All sin begins with a lie. During this study, what specific lies about God's mercy did you discover in your thinking?

_____

_____

_____

_____

_____

How has meditating on God's mercy impacted or changed your **beliefs**?

_____

_____

_____

_____

_____

Value Bible!
Consider what you **want**: How has meditating on God's
mercy revealed misplaced **desires** or **affections**?

_____

_____

_____

_____

_____

Going forward, what steps can you take to better ground
your heart and mind in this truth about God? How will you
intentionally nurture a growing affection for what God loves
and values?

Live Bible!
"You don't really believe something until you believe it
enough to act on it." Obedience is expressed in and with
your body as you yield your will to God. Considering your
recent choices, how can you better respond to God's mercy
with trust, worship, and humble submission?

Consider your **actions**: What step(s) of obedience do you
need to take to demonstrate a yielded **will** to God?

_____

_____

_____

_____

In what practical ways does God want you to demonstrate
the reality of his mercy to those with whom you interact
(family, friends, co-workers, neighbors, etc.)?

_____

_____

_____

_____

My Tree

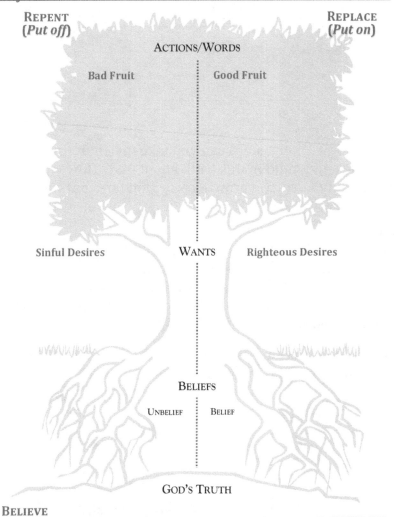

REPENT
(*Put off*)

REPLACE
(*Put on*)

ACTIONS/WORDS

Bad Fruit   Good Fruit

Sinful Desires   WANTS   Righteous Desires

BELIEFS

UNBELIEF : BELIEF

GOD'S TRUTH

BELIEVE

God says . . . I submit to it!

God is . . . I believe it!

Share

Share what you are learning with God through prayer. Although he already knows, it is good to take time to respond to him— praising him for who he is (God is *always* the Lord of mercy!) and asking for his enabling to grow in the areas where the Spirit has convicted you. Write out a simple prayer to God in the space below:

_____

_____

_____

_____

_____

_____

_____

_____

_____

_____

_____

_____

_____

_____

_____

_____

_____

_____

Finally, share what you are learning with other believers. Rejoice together in the truth about God! Encourage one another toward Christlikeness. Humbly open yourself up for accountability.

Appendix

"It remains for us to think on these truths and pray over them until they begin to glow in us. If we cooperate with him in loving obedience, God will manifest Himself to us, and that manifestation will be the difference between a nominal Christian life and a life radiant with the light of his face."

A.W. Tozer

The Tree

Luke 6:43-49

Jesus used a simple word picture to illustrate an important truth about people. Just as a tree shows its nature by the fruit it produces, the inner nature of a person—what he wants and what he believes—is revealed by the fruit—the actions and words—produced in his life.

Luke 6:43-45
For a good tree bringeth not forth corrupt fruit; neither doth a corrupt tree bring forth good fruit. For every tree is known by his own fruit. For of thorns men do not gather figs, nor of a bramble bush gather they grapes. A good man out of the good treasure of his heart bringeth forth that which is good; and an evil man out of the evil treasure of his heart bringeth forth that which is evil: for of the abundance of the heart his mouth speaketh.

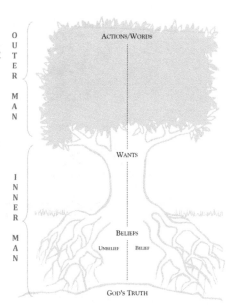

This simple illustration gives us so much hope because it shows us that true, lasting change is really possible. But not by just trying to change fruit—taking off the bad and replacing it with good. This kind of change is superficial and won't last. Next season, the same bad fruit will grow again because the tree hasn't really changed. As seen in the diagram above, a deeper change is needed. We need God to expose the sin in our inner man—our sinful desires and our wrong beliefs about him. Real change begins when we cry out to him, "Lord, change my tree!" Repentance on this level that comes from knowing God will result in righteous desires and fruit that brings glory to God.

---

[17] The Tree explanation and diagrams copyright © 2020 by The Wilds. Used by permission.

An understanding of how our *actions* (what we do, say, and think) are tied to what we *believe* helps us begin the process of real and lasting change:

- We believe a lie about God. *(Beliefs)*
- That unbelief influences our desires. *(Wants)*
- Ungodly desires motivate us to act in sinful ways. *(Actions)*

In summary: *You do what you do, and you say what you say, because you want what you want. You want what you want because you believe what you believe about God, about his Word, and about yourself.*

We always please the one we love the most. So, our actions reveal who/what we love. Every sin struggle reveals this process.

Since the root of every sin is *unbelief*, changing the character of our "tree" means we must know and *believe* the truth about God. This is the most important aspect of biblical change: beholding the glory of God. As we "behold" him in his Word, we are gradually changed to reflect his glory.

> *2 Corinthians 3:18 But we all, with open face beholding as in a glass the glory of the Lord, are changed into the same image from glory to glory, even as by the Spirit of the Lord.*

This might sound simplistic, but God doesn't make it complicated. The ultimate answer to the difficult problems of life is as simple as the gospel: repent and believe.

With God's help (because we can't do it on our own) we must "put off" what is not like Christ in our lives (both in the outer and inner man). **Repent** of unbelief. Identify and reject the lies we have chosen to believe about God, and replace them with truth. Receive God's Word, submitting to what he says in humble obedience. Prayerfully read and study the Bible to discover the truth about God, and specifically, what he thinks about our sin. Rather than just seeking principles, look for a Person. What does God say about Himself? What do we need to begin believing about his character? Memorize and prayerfully meditate on his Word until it changes us from the inside out (2 Cor. 3:18; Ps. 119:9-11; Pr. 2:1-5; Eph. 5:26). **Believe** what God says. Believers are able to trust what the Bible reveals about God's character. The Bible call this process the renewing of our minds (Eph. 4:23).

Repent of sinful desires and disobedient actions. Biblical repentance includes confessing sin to God and forsaking it (Pr. 28:13; 1 Jn. 1:9); seeking forgiveness from others and making restitution (Acts 24:16; Mt. 5:23-25); and cutting off sin at its source by radically removing it from our lives (Mt. 5:28-30; Col. 3:5-7). With God's help (because we can't do it on our own) we must "put on" righteous desires and actions—seeking to imitate the character of Christ (Rom. 12:1-2; 13:14). New patterns of godly thinking and righteous affections are developed over time as the Spirit works within us, opening our eyes to God's glory and producing in us *reverence* and *love* for him that leads to *obedience* from the heart (Rom. 6:17). This requires a personal commitment to "behold" God—reading, studying, memorizing, and meditating on God's Word with the intent to obey in the power of God's Spirit. When we believe God's words and trust his character it will be demonstrated by the fruit of obedience in our lives. God has provided the local church where other believers help us in the process of growth. It is wise to invite accountability. Who can help us become more like Jesus (Eccl. 4:9-12; Pr. 27:5-6)?

The diagram on the following page shows this process of change described in Ephesians 4. Put off. Renew. Put on.

This is God's design for change to take place in our lives. There is no plan B. God has promised to make each of his children like his Son, and he will not fail in this task! He is changing us through our relationship with Christ. By God's grace, we can see lasting change by choosing to believe God and choosing to live out that belief in loving, dependent obedience.

The examples that follow in this booklet illustrate the outer and inner man in a variety of common sin struggles. They present possible actions, desires, and beliefs that may be present in the life of someone choosing a particular sin. While not exhaustive, these examples are intended to help get to the deeper level of a problem where change ultimately needs to take place.

Put off   ACTIONS/WORDS   *Put on*

Confess & Forsake   **Accountability**
Proverbs 28:13   Ecclesiastes 4:9-12
I John 1:9   Proverbs 27:5-6

Forgiveness Asked/
Restitution Made   **Replacement**
Acts 24:16   Romans 12:21
Matthew 5:23-25   Romans 13:14

                              WANTS

        Radical Removal
        Matthew 5:28-30
        Colossians 3:5-7

                              BELIEFS

                    UNBELIEF   BELIEF

                         GOD'S TRUTH
                         Renew
                  Read/Study/Memorize
                      Meditate/Apply
                     2 Corinthians 3:18
                        I John 3:1-3

The Tree

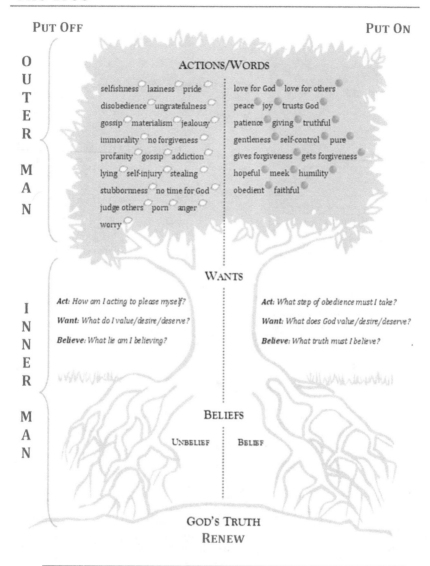

OUTER MAN

ACTIONS/WORDS

PUT OFF	PUT ON
selfishness laziness pride	love for God love for others
disobedience ungratefulness	peace joy trusts God
gossip materialism jealousy	patience giving truthful
immorality no forgiveness	gentleness self-control pure
profanity gossip addiction	gives forgiveness gets forgiveness
lying self-injury stealing	hopeful meek humility
stubbornness no time for God	obedient faithful
judge others porn anger	
worry	

INNER MAN

WANTS

Act: How am I acting to please myself?

Want: What do I value/desire/deserve?

Believe: What lie am I believing?

Act: What step of obedience must I take?

Want: What does God value/desire/deserve?

Believe: What truth must I believe?

BELIEFS

UNBELIEF   BELIEF

GOD'S TRUTH
RENEW

I do what I do, and I say what I say, because I want what I want.
I want what I want because I believe what I believe
about God, about His Word, and about myself.

Questions That Draw Out The Heart

It is possible for people to have similar fruit with very different desires and beliefs fueling the growth of that fruit. How can a counselor understand what desires and beliefs produced the observable words and actions in the "outer man"? A counselor must ask questions. Good questions that are thoughtful, gracious, relevant, and open-ended help draw out the heart (Pr. 20:5). Ask questions to help identify what the counselee wants so badly that he has given himself permission to make a sinful choice.

QUESTIONS THAT DRAW OUT DESIRES:
What is it you want so badly, value so highly, or deserve so much that you are willing to sin to try to get it? What ruling desire is fueling your choice to act in disobedience to God's revealed Word and character (1 Jn. 2:15-17)? While not comprehensive, the categories below provide examples of desires that are "common to man" (1 Cor. 10:13). Questions like these can help you identify the desires of the heart you are seeking to satisfy by your sin.

- *Security: What or whom are you trusting in for safety and security instead of God? What do you fear losing or worry about not having?*
- *Pleasure: What do you like about your sin? In what ways does this sin comfort or make you feel good?*
- *Possessions: What possession do you value so much that you are willing to pursue it above Christ in your life? How does what you "own" contribute to your sense of worth or well-being?*
- *Significance: Is there a certain position that you value so highly you are willing to sin to get it or keep it? In what ways does your sin make you feel important, noticed, or cared for by others?*
- *Control: In what ways does your sin give you a sense of being "in control"? What harmful outcome do you fear by not being in control?*

A counselor must take his questions another level deeper still, because the desires that influence a counselee's sinful actions originate from unbelief. We don't simply fall into sin. Our minds think a certain way about ourselves, others, and God. The lies we think and believe fuel our desire for sin. Biblical change will impact the **mind** (what we think), the **affections** (what we want) and the **will** (what we choose).

QUESTIONS THAT DRAW OUT BELIEF:
- *Capture your thinking: What were you thinking when you chose to sin? What excuses or arguments did you use to justify your sin?*
- *Classify your thinking: Were you thinking truth? In what way did your thinking differ from what God values and says in his Word? What lies have you believed?*
- *Correct your thinking: What aspect of God's character have you been reflecting? What truth about God do you need to start believing?*

Anger/Bitterness

PUT OFF   **PUT ON**

ACTIONS/WORDS

Bad Fruit:
- Revenge and retaliation
- Violent outbursts
- Bitterness
- Selfish pouting
- Hurtful words
- Resenting people
- Will not forgive

Good Fruit:
- Forgiveness
- Contentment with what I have/don't have
- Self-control
- Patient and kind speech
- Peace with God and others

Sinful Desires: WANTS   **Righteous Desires:**
- I *deserve* to have my own way!
- I *want* to punish those who hurt me.
- I *want* control.

- I *want* to submit to God's way.
- I *value* reconciliation because of the gospel.
- I *want* to show love and mercy to those who hurt me.

BELIEFS

UNBELIEF BELIEF

GOD'S TRUTH

RENEW

God says...

James 1:19-20; Ephesians 4:26, 31; Proverbs 16:32; Hebrews 12:14-15

God is...

God is All-knowing. God is Gracious. God is Merciful/Patient. God is Love. God is Righteous/Just.

Worry/Fear/Anxiety

PUT OFF   PUT ON

ACTIONS/WORDS

Bad Fruit:

- Obsessive/compulsive behavior
- "What if"/"if only" thinking
- Insomnia
- Hoarding

Good Fruit:

- Gratitude to God/others
- "Think Bible"
- Bringing concerns to God in prayer
- Emotional stability

Sinful Desires:

WANTS

Righteous Desires:

- I *want* to be in control.
- I *want* to solve every problem ahead of time.
- I *value* comfort at any cost.

- I *want* to trust God's control.
- I *value* the genuine comfort that God provides.
- I *want* to live in the reality of

BELIEFS

UNBELIEF   BELIEF

GOD'S TRUTH

RENEW

God says...

Psalm 55:22; Matthew 6:25-34; Philippians 4:4-7; 1 John 4:16-19; Hebrews 13:5-6

God is...

God is All-powerful. God is Faithful. God is Good. God is Sovereign/In Control. God is Sufficient.

God is...

God is...	Definition	Scripture
All-knowing	God fully knows all things—past, present, and future.	Pr. 15:3 Mt. 10:30
All-powerful	God is free and able to do whatever He wills.	Jer. 32:17 Ps. 115:3
All-present	God is present everywhere at all times.	1 Kgs. 8:27 Jer. 23:23-24
Beauty	God is altogether lovely. He defines what is beautiful.	Ps. 27:4 Job 40:2, 10
Faithful	God is reliable. God will always do what He has said and fulfill what He has promised.	Nu. 23:19 Dt. 7:9 2 Tim. 2:13
Good	God is the final standard of good, and all that He does is worthy of approval.	Ps. 34:8 Lk. 18:19
Grace	God gives kindness towards those who do not deserve it.	Eph. 2:7-9 Tit. 2:11
Holy	God is absolutely pure. He is separate from all that is unclean and evil.	1 Jn. 1:5 Ps. 99:9
Immutable	God's nature is absolutely unchangeable. He cannot change because He is perfect. He is always the same.	Mal. 3:6 Heb. 13:8
Jealous	God earnestly seeks to protect His own honor. Only God deserves honor and glory.	Isa. 42:8 Ex. 34:14

The only way to change "bad fruit" into "good fruit" is to become a "good tree" (Psalm 1). The way to become a good tree is by prayerfully reading and studying the Bible to learn about the character of God. The more you get to know God, the more you will learn to trust Him.

God is...

God is...	Definition	Scripture
Love	God eternally gives of Himself for the good of others. He always does the sacrificial thing towards others.	1 Jn. 4:7-8 Jn. 3:16 Rom. 5:8
Merciful/ Patient	God is slow to anger, not giving us the punishment that we deserve.	Ps. 103:8 Isa. 55:7
Order (Peace)	God is separate from all confusion and disorder.	1 Cor. 14:33 Col. 3:15
Righteous/ Just	God is the final standard of what is right. He will always punish the wicked and reward the righteous without favoritism.	Ps. 19:9 Acts 17:31
Sovereign/ In Control	God rules over His creation. He actively guides all events to fulfill His purpose.	Isa. 46:9-10 Pr. 21:1
Sufficient	God is more than enough. He alone satisfies.	Heb. 13:5 2 Cor. 3:5
Supreme	God is first, above all, chief, and supreme.	Col. 1:16-18 1 Cor. 8:6
Truth	God is the source of all truth. He cannot lie for what He says is real and true.	Nu. 23:19 1 Jn. 5:20
Wisdom	God always chooses the best goals and the best ways to reach those goals.	Rom. 11:33 Job 9:2-4

This chart is designed to give an overview of various aspects of God's nature and can be used as a starting point for further study of God's attributes. As you prayerfully seek to know God, you can be confident in His promise to "change your tree."

The Inductive Study Method

There is a big difference between an "inductive" and a "deductive" approach to Bible study. Inductive simply means that you come to the Bible with the desire to examine what the Bible says *before* you decide what the Bible says. Like a good scientist, you thoroughly investigate all the facts before drawing any conclusions. In contrast, a deductive approach to Bible study means that you come to the Bible with preconceived ideas *already* formed, looking for Scripture to support your position. We will often come away with wrong ideas about God, his world, and ourselves when we approach the Bible this way. It is important that you allow God's Word to speak for itself. Of course, unlike a scientist who studies the natural world, we cannot understand spiritual truth using our own intellect. We need God to open our eyes to his truth. This is dependent work!

Choose a passage or verse you would like to study. Get out your Bible, a notebook, and something with which to write. Use the guide below to dig deep into the passage (elements of this guide were taken from *A Place of Quiet Rest* by Nancy Leigh DeMoss). Don't rush. Take several days to slowly and prayerfully work through each of the three big questions:

1. *What does it say?*
2. *What does it mean?*
3. *What should I do?*

You don't have to follow every detail listed below—simply use the basic elements of the inductive study method as a guide, at whatever level you feel comfortable. God honors those who seek him with a tender, humble heart. Record what you learn in a notebook.

PREPARATION: *Getting My Heart Ready to Meet with God*
As you open the Word, continually express your dependence on God to help you to understand his Word. Prayer is our

humble way of demonstrating that we know we can't "get it" on our own. Ask God to give you a tender and humble heart that is eager to obey whatever he shows you in his Word. In our family we like to call it "obedient listening."

> **Psalm 25:4-5** *Make me to know your ways, O LORD; teach me your paths. Lead me in your truth and teach me, for you are the God of my salvation; for you I wait all the day long.*

OBSERVATION: *What Does It Say?*
Start with the most obvious, simple observations about the passage before probing deeper for further understanding.

Simple Observations:
1. Consider the **context** ("con" = together; "textus" = woven) of the verse/passage. When we open the Bible to one particular chapter of one particular book, that chapter is connected to what comes before it and what comes after it. Context matters! How is this verse/passage connected to what comes before and after it? Record what you learn.
2. Ask **investigative questions** such as who, what, when, where, why, and how. Record what you discover.
   - *Who* wrote it? To whom was it written?
   - *What* happened? What are the main events?
   - *When* was it written? When did the events take place?
   - *Where* did it happen? Where is the author/the audience?
   - *Why* was this written?
   - *How* did it happen? How is the audience expected to respond?
3. Look for patterns—**repeated words, phrases, or ideas** to help you understand what the author intends to emphasize. It might be helpful to mark these patterns with a colored pencil or highlighter.
4. Look for the **author's purpose**. Who is writing? Who is he writing to? What is the situation? What problems are being addressed? Is there a single idea that holds everything together? Finding the answers to these

questions will help you answer the bigger question, "Why did the author write this?" Apply this same question to God Himself, remembering that he is the ultimate Author!
5. Try to locate the key verse of the passage.
6. Consider **genre** (Is this section of Scripture historical narrative, poetry, prophecy, epistle, or apocalyptic?). The genres often mix together, and this can sometimes be confusing. Wherever you happen to be studying, always look for God's character—he is the unifying theme throughout all types of genres.

Deeper Digging:
1. Look up the meaning of **key words** in the passage. Don't worry about finding something profound for every word; just look for the essential meaning of the main words in the passage. It is best to look up the definition in the original languages rather than English. There are many good resources available to help with this process such as *Blue Letter Bible* and *Olive Tree*. These websites allow the user to look up word definitions as well as dig into the grammar of the Greek and Hebrew words (part of speech, tense, voice, etc.). It is easier than it sounds! (For helpful tutorials, go to www.blueletterbible.org/help/videoHelps.cfm#section3.) The word definitions listed will give you a general idea of the word's meaning. When several definitions are given for a word, you may wonder, "Which definition do I pick?" A word study dictionary, such as Vine's, will often give a very specific meaning for the exact verse you are studying. But you may have to look up other verses that use the same word to see how it is used in other parts of the Bible. Look back at the context of your passage and consider which definition fits best. Sometimes you just have to prayerfully wrestle with it—this is called meditation.
2. Look for **"linking words."** Linking words help us see the flow of an argument, reveal the connection between different statements, or point our attention to a result.

- Some linking words point **forward**: *therefore, consequently, for this reason, thus.* These words take what has come before and point your attention toward a conclusion that is coming. They usually tell us about a result or consequence that flows from the previous statement. (Examples: Matt. 10:16; Phil. 2:6-9; 2 Cor. 4:7)
- Some linking words point **backwards**: *for, because, since, so.* In those cases, the reason or explanation comes after that word. (Example: Heb. 4:14-15)
- The linking phrase *"so that"* tells us the purpose or result of something. (Examples: Phil. 2:10; 1 Jn. 2:1; 2 Cor. 4:7)

3. Look up **cross-references** to provide a broader understanding of the verse/passage. You can find other related Scripture passages in the margin of your Bible, the concordance located in the back of your Bible, or by using the search feature in an online Bible program. Write down any insights you gain that help you better understand your topic.
4. Read the passage in various translations.
5. Using the information you have gathered so far, take time to summarize the "big idea" of the passage in your own words.
6. After spending personal time in study and meditation on the passage, you may want to consult some trusted commentaries or the notes in a study Bible to gain further insight.

INTERPRETATION: *What Does It Mean?*
The goal of studying the Bible is to understand what God has communicated about himself so that we can know and glorify him (Col. 1:9-10). Remember, the Bible is all about a Person! Good interpretation seeks to get at the plain meaning of God's Word. Ask the following kinds of questions to better understand the meaning of the text. Journal your thoughts.

- What does this passage teach me about God the Father, Jesus, or the Holy Spirit?
- What does this passage teach me about myself?
- Are there any promises to claim (stated or implied)?
- Are there any commands to obey (stated or implied)?

APPLICATION: *What Should I Do?*
Application asks the question, "What should I do with the truth I've seen?" As you read and study the Bible, ask the Lord to help you apply what you learn to everyday life. What needs to change so that your life better reflects God's character? This step should help you move past just **hearing** God's Word to actually **doing** it! Making truth practical means going beyond **general** application (which is fairly simple and non-confrontive: (*"I need to pray more"*) and actually getting very **specific** (*"I will demonstrate my dependence on God by starting each day in prayer"*).

Prayerfully consider what specific **action steps** you need to take in response to what God has shown you in his Word. Plan to use what you learn. Application is often the hardest step of Bible study. It forces us to be honest with ourselves and with God. Use probing questions, like the ones below, to help you personalize what you are learning. Ask God to enable you to have a whole-hearted response to his Word (Ps. 119:2, 10): A "whole heart" includes your mind, desires, and will. While application is often a humbling step, it also prepares us to receive grace from God (Js. 4:6)!

- Consider your relationship with **God**. *How does knowing God change me?*
- Think about your relationships with **others**. *How does knowing God change the way I relate to others?*
- **Think Bible**: *How does meditating on God's truth impact or change your **beliefs**?*
- **Value Bible**: *How does meditating on God's truth correct your misplaced **desires** or **affections**?*
- **Live Bible**: *What steps of obedience do you need to take to demonstrate a yielded **will** to God?*

Having God expose sin and bring conviction in your life can be a humbling experience, but it is one of the most loving things that he does for you. Like a doctor who tells you the truth about a serious illness in your body, God wants you to understand the incredibly destructive nature of sin in your life. But the good news is that he also provides the cure: **the gospel.**

The gospel reminds you that just as Christ died in your place, he also obeyed in your place. He is your justification and he is your sanctification. Becoming like Jesus means far more than just imitating him. Becoming like Jesus means that his life in you becomes more and more of a reality in your daily experience (Gal. 2:20). This is why it is so important to think about the gospel every day.

You never can and never will earn God's favor by how well you perform. As a believer you never have to fear the loss of your righteous standing before God. You will always and only relate to God through Jesus on the basis of his finished work on your behalf. And this means that you are free to face your sin because you don't ever have to fear facing God's wrath. *So apply God's truth to your life with gospel hope, trusting him to help you obey as you humbly depend on him.*

Take time to **respond to God** in prayer and worship. Consider writing out your response in the form of a prayer. In this prayer, you might confess and repent of sin, ask for help to change, offer praise to the One Who is worthy, or all of the above!

Finally, do you need accountability in this area? Share what you are learning with another believer. Transparent, humble sharing helps cement truth in our hearts and mobilizes helpful **accountability**.

Word Study Tools

In every passage you set out to study, there are certain key words that unlock the meaning. Further study of those words using some of the following tools can be very helpful.

Bible Dictionaries/Bible Encyclopedias
Give background about people, places, or things that we find in the Bible.

Bible Lexicons
Help us understand the meaning and source of words found in the Bible.

Bible Grammar Helps
Provide a fuller understanding of the grammatical structure and meaning of words found in the Bible.

Bible Commentaries
A good commentary that stays close to the meaning of the text will do a lot of digging for you.

Caution: A commentary is not inspired, and even good men can be wrong. Avoid looking at the comments of other people until you have done your own study.

Bible Software Programs
A good Bible software program incorporates all of the word study tools listed above and makes Bible study much simpler.

Suggested Resources

Concordances

Strong, James. *The New Strong's Exhaustive Concordance of the Bible: Classic Edition*. Nelson Reference, 1991.

Young, Robert. *Young's Analytical Concordance to the Bible*. Hendrickson Publishers, 1984.

Bible Dictionaries

Wood, D.R. W. et al. *New Bible Dictionary*. InterVarsity Press, 1996.

Douglas, J.D., and Merrill C. Tenney. *Zondervan's Pictorial Bible Dictionary*. Zondervan, 1999.

Unger, Merrill Frederick, and R. K. Harrison. *The New Unger's Bible Dictionary*. Moody Publishers, 1988.

Bible Encyclopedias

Tenney, Merrill C. *Zondervan Pictorial Encyclopedia of the Bible*, Vols. 1-5. Zondervan, 1975.

Orr, James et al. *The International Standard Bible Encyclopedia*. Hendrickson Publishers, 1994.

Bromiley, Geoffery W. *The International Standard Bible Encyclopedia: 4 Vol. Set*. Wm. B. Eerdmans Publishing Company, 1998.

Study Bibles

Arthur, K. and Precept Ministries. *The International Inductive Study Bible*. Harvest House Publishers, 1993.

MacArthur, John. *The MacArthur Study Bible*. Nelson Bibles, 1997.

Zodhiates, Spiros. *The Hebrew-Greek Key Word Study Bible*. AMG Publishers, 1998.

Single Volume Commentaries

Walvoord. *Bible Knowledge Commentary Old Testament and New Testament*. Victor Books, 1985.

Carson, D.A. et al. *New Bible Commentary: 21st Century Edition*. InterVarsity Press, 1994.

Dockery, *David S. Holman Concise Bible Commentary*. Broadman and Holman, 1998.

Multi-volume Commentary Sets

Gaebelein, Frank E. *Expositor's Bible Commentary 7-Volume Old Testament Set*, Zondervan, 1992. Also *Expositor's Bible Commentary 5-Volume New Testament Set*. Zondervan, 1982.

Henry, Matthew. *Commentary on the Whole Bible, 6-Volume Set*. (Free online at www.studylight.org.)

Morris, Leon. *Tyndale New Testament Commentaries*. Wm. B. Eerdmans

Publishing Company, 1965.

Greek Word Study Books
Vine, W.E., and Merrill F. Unger. *Vine's Complete Expository Dictionary of Old and New Testament Words*: With Topical Index. Nelson Reference, 1996.

Thayer, Joseph. *Thayer's Greek-English Lexicon of the New Testament*: Coded with Strong's Concordance Numbers. Hendrickson Publishers, 1996.

Zodhiates, Spiros. *The Complete Word Study Dictionary: New Testament (Word Study Series)*. AMG Publishers, 1992.

Hebrew Word Study Books
Harris, R. Laird et al. *Theological Wordbook of the Old Testament (2-vol. Set)*. Moody Publishers, 1980. (Keyed to Strong's numbers.)

Baker, Warren. *The Complete Word Study Dictionary: Old Testament (Word Study)*. AMG Publishers, 2003.

The Brown Driver Briggs Hebrew and English Lexicon. Hendrickson Publishers, 2000 (5th printing). (Keyed to Strong's numbers.)

Software Collections
Power Bible
Logos
Bibleworks
Quickverse
eBible

Resources on the Web
www.blueletterbible.org
www.studylight.org
www.esword.net
www.onlinebible.com
www.studylight.org

The following pages are excerpts from my personal time with the Lord spent considering this extended passage on the supremacy of God. For sake of space, I didn't include everything, just a sampling to give you an idea of how to go about this type of study on your own. It came straight from my journal—so you won't find complete sentences or proper grammar— just my thoughts on paper. I never intended to share this with anyone, but I hope that doing so will help you understand the inductive study process a little better.

This particular passage took me several weeks to study through. I would tackle just a little bit at a time—spending several of my personal devotion times just considering the context, then moving on to simple observations as I took several more days to just read the passage through again and again. When I got to the word studies, I just looked up a few words each day. Little by little I built my own commentary on the passage. And all along the way, I recorded what God taught me about himself and what he wanted me to change in my life. There is no need to rush in Bible study. Consider taking the challenge to stay in one place, digging deep, until God shows you himself. It's worth the wait and the patient time spent in meditation!

God is Supreme: God is first, above all, chief, and supreme.

1 Corinthians 8:6
Yet for us there is one God, the Father, from whom are all things and for whom we exist, and one Lord, Jesus Christ, through whom are all things and through whom we exist.

OBSERVATION: *What does God say about himself?*

Context/Observations:
When you begin an in-depth study in a passage, it is often helpful to read about the background and themes of the book in the introduction to that particular book in a good

study Bible. This will give you a quick overview and help with understanding the context and setting of the verse(s) you are about to study. Knowing who the passage was written to and why it was written can add much to your understanding of what God is communicating to his people. Read the surrounding verses, or even the whole chapter, several times and record what you learn from a surface overview of the text. How is this verse/passage connected to what comes before and after it? Below are my observations from 1 Corinthians 8:6.

> Paul is writing to the church in Corinth about some very serious issues in their local church body. Corinth was one of the largest and wealthiest cities in the Roman Empire. Very important center of trade and culture. It was a wicked city- and that wickedness had crept into the church- sin, divisions, immorality, lawsuits, confusion, heresy, etc. Probably most of the members were saved out of paganism and had a lot of baggage to overcome.
>
> Chapter 8 specifically deals with eating food that has been offered to idols. This has become an issue in the church. Paul helps them with their theology regarding this cultural issue. (What should the relationship be between a Christian and their surrounding pagan culture?) "Paul wants this church, divided because of the arrogance of its more powerful members, to work together for the advancement of the gospel."
>
> The worship of many different pagan gods was a part of government, trade, society, everyday life. The church has serious problems- like a self-centered insistence on their own rights at the expense of others. Needed to make a clean break from the moral impurity of their culture and start reflecting God's character.
>
> Look for sharp contrasts between truth and error.
>
> Theme of "Know" and "Knowledge" (v. 1)
>
> This is what we know:
>
> - v. 4 -There is <u>no</u> such thing as an idol; there is only One God.
> - vv. 5-6 -Even if there are <u>many</u> gods and lords, for us there

is but <u>one</u> God and <u>one</u> Lord.

- v. 7 -But not all men have this knowledge.
- v.12 -When I sin against my fellow brothers by insisting on my own liberty and wounding their conscience, I actually sin against Christ Himself.
- v. 11 –True knowledge will not ruin others (contrast to "edify" in v. 1)

I can know a lot and still be truly ignorant (v. 2)

Knowledge alone results in arrogance but agape love results in edification (build, profit spiritually, advancement of others).

The important thing is not "what I know" but rather, it is being known by God.

Key Words:
Use a word study tool to find out more about the meanings of key words. Don't worry about finding something profound for every word; just try to discover the essential meaning. I like to use *Blue Letter Bible* because it is so simple, but there are many good resources listed under *Suggested Resources* that will help you easily discover the definitions of the Hebrew or Greek words you are looking for. I did word studies on the whole passage, but for sake of space, I have included just a sampling here to give the general idea. If you have time and want to dig further, you may find it helpful to apply one or more of the tools for Bible study at this point (i.e., the author's purpose, linking words, genre, repetition, etc.).

one = 1520 numerically one, in contrast to "many" (v. 5)

God = 2316 God, singular. Used in verse 5 for heathen gods- but there it is plural. This name is parallel to Elohim used in the OT.

Father = 3962 A first author or beginner of anything. Spoken of God as the Creator; Father of man by creation and by redemption.

from = 1537 out of, from; origin, source; out of which one comes.

for = 1519 motion into any place or thing; opposite of "out of"

(1537). Used often in NT to indicate intention, purpose, identity, aim. (We are "in him" – identified with Christ.)

Lord = 2962 Kurios; wielding authority for good. Contrast with "despotes" – wielding authority over slaves. The owner and possessor of a thing. The one who has the power of deciding.

Christ = 5547 anointed; title given in OT to those anointed in the priesthood or those acting as redeemers.

through = 1223 refers to the channel of an act; through, from, by occasion of, by reason of. I can't exist for him without Jesus Christ- it is "by" him. He is the channel of activity in my life. Without him I can do nothing.

Cross References:

Cross references are "other verses that relate to, confirm, or shed light on" the passage you are studying. You can find cross references listed in the margins of a good study Bible. Or as you look up word definitions, you may find other verses that use the same Greek or Hebrew word. Reading these verses can help provide a broader understanding of the verse/attribute of God you are studying. Write down what you learn.

> **John 1:3** *All things were made through him, and without him was not any thing made that was made.*
> **Acts 17:28-29** *...In him we live and move and have our being.*
> **Romans 11:36** *For from him and through him and to him are all things. To him be glory forever.*
> **Ephesians 4:5-6** *One Lord, one faith, one baptism, one God and Father of all, who is over all and through all and in all.*
> **Colossians 1:16** *For by him all things were created, in heaven and on earth, visible and invisible, whether thrones or dominions or rulers or authorities—all things were created through him and for him.*

Capture the big idea of the passage:

After you are finished with the word studies, take time to go back through the information you have gathered so far and carefully think about what you have learned. Take time to summarize the "big idea" of the passage in your own words.

Depending on the length of the passage, I like to devote at least one full devotional time to this step.

> In contrast to those who believe there are many gods, for me- one who is known by God and belongs to him- there is only one God. The One true God, Elohim, the Father; the Author and Beginner of all things, the Creator, the Origin and Source of all. All things, without exception, find their source in God. This includes us! Our purpose and identity are in him. Our purpose and aim is God Himself- we exist for him! And for me there is One Authority, Jesus the Messiah, anointed by God. He is the reason I even exist.

INTERPRETATION: *What does it mean?*

This step doesn't have to be done all at once. As I am going through a passage and the Lord shows me a significant truth, I write it down right away. I like to keep a running list of what I am learning each day. In a way, this space is for collecting all the points of truth you gather along the way in one place.

If you are following the *Inductive Study Method* sheet, please don't feel like you have to go through all of the questions under this heading. I rarely go through this entire list of questions; they simply help you know what types of things you might be looking for as you seek to discern what this passage means. Here are the truths I gathered from 1 Corinthians 8:6:

- Man has created thousands upon thousands of idols to worship since the beginning of time. These are all false, pretender gods. There is only One God and he alone is worthy of worship.
- God created us- we exist by him and for him- not the other way around. Idols are created by man and they "exist" to do things for man. Our relationship to God is completely different. But it is so easy to slip into the mindset that he exists "for us."
- Idols have no power of their own- their existence is completely reliant upon their maker.

- This passage reminds us that God and Jesus are one and the same, equal. Jesus shares this place of ultimate supremacy, "One God, the Father...One Lord, Jesus Christ."
- In this passage Paul is especially addressing their flippant disregard for others. They are exercising their liberty without thought of how it affects fellow believers. Even though we have this knowledge that idols are false and there is only one true God, it should not produce in us arrogance (8:1) or disregard for others (8:9-12). Exercising our liberty can actually lead us to sin against our brothers and Christ Himself. Remember who is supreme- it is God, not me!
- Being "known by him" – this is truly vital!
- God's position of supremacy is never threatened. He holds first place securely, unmoving- even if people don't recognize it. He is supreme whether I believe it or not. The goal is to live my life in light of this unshakeable reality.
- "From whom are all things" – all things come from him. That not only means he created all things, it means that all things in this life come from him as well. As Chief, First in all the universe, he has a right to rule and decide.
- My purpose and aim is God Himself- to be fully identified with him in the very reason for my existence. That means all parts of me- will, intellect, emotion, etc. Spiritual and physical are to be aimed at living for him. He is chief and first in importance- not me, my will or my desires.
- Not only do I exist for him, I exist through him. How foolish to act as if I am an independent being. I can't live and move and breathe apart from him. My very existence relies upon him. And certainly this is true in an eternal way as well. Eternal life is completely dependent on him.
- As a Christian there is only one recognized authority in my life- Jesus Christ Himself. I am not the authority. Christ is no despot. He always wields that authority for my benefit.

APPLICATION: *What should I do?*

As with Interpretation, I like to keep a running list of what God is showing me personally as I go through the study day by day. If I leave it for later, I usually forget! Personally, I think application is one of the hardest parts of Bible study. I love it when God opens my eyes to truth! But it isn't quite as exciting to bring that truth down to where I live on a daily basis. Honestly evaluating my life in light of what God is showing me about himself is often painful. This step requires humility and a transparent heart. Tough stuff; but this is where true change really starts to happen! Don't neglect this step. You may want to spend several days reviewing your study and asking God to show you what you should do in response. Here were my actions steps based on the times I spent in 1 Corinthians 8:6:

- When making decisions about Christian liberty (what I have freedom to take part in), make this a foundational consideration: God's Supremacy. I exist for him, not for self- he is Supreme, not me. And his will and the edification of his people is the important thing- not what I want or enjoy. Use this passage when teaching our kids how to make discerning choices.
- Check my heart attitude often for the "God as a man-made idol" kind of thinking. I did not fashion him, he fashioned me. He does not exist to do my bidding, I exist for him and by him and through him. Be conscious of this truth especially when I pray. He is not a genie in a lamp; he is the Supreme God who rules the universe.
- Worship God. If God is Supreme- and he is- then he is the only one I should be worshiping. What do I put in his place? Worship him even when no one else is watching. Even when it seems he is not supreme and life appears out of control. By faith, worship him. This is an important part of living out my belief- rejoicing in his position as first and chief in the universe while I am in the "mothering trenches" at home. Doing this in the daily little things will have a great impact on how I view my ministry at home. God's will and desires are chief, above all else in importance. Embracing that truth in private worship will help me live it out in daily life.
- Be grateful I only have one God- I don't have many gods to try and appease. And my God tells me what he is like and what is pleasing to him. No surprises.

- Repent of my insubordination whenever God shows me that I am seeking to be first and set myself in a position above him or set my desires before him in importance.
- He is my Master- but there are often areas that I do not want to allow under his control. Ask God to bring these to my attention.
- "For whose service we exist." Evaluate regularly- am I living like an owner or a servant/steward? Do a deeper study on this topic.

RESPONDING TO GOD

For many years I did not record my prayers to God. However, I'm glad someone encouraged me to add this step! I have found it extremely beneficial to write out my prayers. Bible study is a two-way communication—listening to God as he speaks to you and then responding to him. I love to go back years later and read what I wrote in this section. It is a good indicator of spiritual growth and so special to be reminded of God's great care in dealing with my heart on a personal level.

> Lord, I worship You, the Supreme God, Highest, Chief, above all, first in all things. I praise You because You are the Originator, Creator, Designer, Source of all things- including me! You alone are worthy of my worship for You alone are God- the Only God- there is no other. I praise You because You are the Lord, the supreme Authority, the Messiah. I praise you for wielding that authority for my good. Thank You that Your purposes and designs are always benevolent. I praise You that You alone hold this position of authority- it is unrivaled, unshakeable, certain. I praise You for creating and sustaining me. My very existence is dependent upon You. Apart from You I can truly do nothing.

> I recognize that I exist for You. This is the very reason You created me. I want to align my life to the reality of Your supremacy. So often I find myself resisting Your authority and being insubordinate in wanting to put my will and desires first. Please forgive me for my rebellion and pride. I exist for You- please help me live with this as my very purpose and

aim. Forgive me for often thinking it should be the other way around and praying with the expectation that You are here to do my bidding. And please forgive me for seeking to live independently of Your sustaining support. Thank you for covering my sin. And thank you for exposing it in the first place. You are so gracious! I love You!